Growing Old Together:
A Serious Comical Devotional for Married Couples

By John M. Cimbala

Dedication

To Suzy.

Thank you for putting up with me for almost forty years! You have made me a better person, and I thank the Lord Jesus Christ that we can pray together and also laugh together.

He who finds a wife finds a good thing and obtains favor from the Lord.
Proverbs 18:22 (ESV).

Acknowledgments

*But we ought always to thank God for you, brothers and sisters loved by
the Lord.*
2 Thessalonians 2:13 (NIV)

Several friends and family members critiqued and edited this book in its first drafts, and I would like to thank them for their many useful corrections, especially regarding Biblical accuracy and grammar, and for spotting typographical errors. I also appreciate their comments, suggestions, and encouragements. I list in alphabetical order those who helped: **Julie Boyette**, **Glen and Patty Coates**, **Helen Dickey**, **John and Leigh Pitterle**, **John Torczynski**, and **Deb Weeks**. I particularly appreciate John Torczynski's meticulous editing of my grammar, especially comma placement, for Julie Boyette's "eagle eye" for spotting typo errors, and for Deb Weeks' wonderful suggestions in analyzing and interpreting context and content from the female perspective.

Finally, I am deeply grateful to my sweet sister **Helen Dickey** for helping me create the two characters, Frank and Ethel, and for drawing them for me. I thank the Lord for her artistic gift and her willingness to share it.

Table of Contents

Forward

A joyful heart is good medicine.
Proverbs 17:22 (ESV)

This book is based on a collection of comical conversations between a fictional married couple, Frank and Ethel Grolto, who are growing old together. I posted one of these comics on Facebook every week for about three years. Some friends urged me to collect the comics into a book. So… here it is! I added a devotional to each comic so that a husband and wife (*together*) can laugh at the comic, read the devotional and Bible passage, discuss some serious issues, and pray with each other. My goal for this book is that couples draw closer to each other, and in the process draw closer to the Lord. There are 52 devotionals, one per week for a year. I suggest scheduling a half hour when you can sit together and go through a devotional. Some couples may wish to split up the devotional into two shorter time slots – whatever works best for your schedules. In particular, the **Study Together** section can be postponed to a later time during the week if you cannot complete the full devotional in one sitting.

The devotionals are original. However, I cannot claim that all the comical conversations are original. Some of the comics are based on jokes, movies, or comics that I recalled from years ago and "massaged" into the present format. I don't give references because I cannot be sure from what source the ideas originated. Much of the inspiration came from actual conversations with my wife. I changed the wording here and there, however, to make the comics more readable and/or humorous. I confess that most of these conversations are entirely made up. I tried my best to tie the devotionals and scripture references to the comical conversations.

Every one of the comics and devotionals is "clean" (no foul language and nothing of an overtly sexual nature). As a Christian, I want to please the Lord Jesus Christ in my authoring. I believe that God has a great sense of humor and has given people the ability to laugh along with him.

I pray that you will benefit from and enjoy these devotionals!

John M. Cimbala, 26 June 2019

Meet Frank and Ethel Grolto

Frank and **Ethel Grolto**[1] are in their early 60s and have been married for almost 40 years. Age is beginning to take its toll both physically and mentally, but they always manage to find humor in growing old together. They have two adult children and are beginning to be blessed with grandchildren. They are devoted to each other in the covenant of marriage and have a strong Christian faith. They pray together each day and are always looking for new, exciting, and fun but serious marriage-related devotionals.

Frank is a balding, absentminded Professor of Engineering, nearing retirement. In addition to teaching college classes, he also writes textbooks, Bible study material, and Christian-themed books. Frank thinks social media is only for family pictures, humor, and Christian witnessing. He is overly concerned about how old he looks. High on his bucket list is that one of his books, videos, or social media posts goes viral. You would think that after nearly 40 years of marriage Frank would understand women, but he is often clueless.

---

[1] Any similarities to John and Suzy Cimbala are purely coincidental.

Ethel is a retired nurse who is now a homemaker, having raised their two children. She manages the home, loves to cook, and tries to keep Frank in line. She doesn't think Frank is as funny as *he* thinks he is. Ethel has a quick wit and occasionally comes up with some great one-liners. While Frank is still struggling to understand women, Ethel understood men even before she married Frank.

Foundational Bookend. Covenant

First Devotional (not a laughing matter):

Ethel: (reflecting) Do you realize
we have been married for
almost 40 years?
Frank: Wow! Why did you stick
with me all these years?
Ethel: Because when I said,
"I do" to you, I said,
"I don't" to everyone else!
Frank: ♥...☺
Ethel: ☺...♥

Artwork by Helen Dickey

Take care, lest you forget the covenant of the LORD your God, which he made with you.
Deuteronomy 4:23 (ESV)

Read Together:

The first and last devotionals in this book are "bookends." This first one is foundational and sets the theme for the rest of the devotionals.

The definition of ***covenant*** is "an agreement, usually formal, between two persons to do or not do something specified." Marriage is a great example of a covenant. It is a formal agreement between a man and a woman to do or not do something specified, as in the above definition. We see this clearly in the marriage vows: both persons agree to *love each other till death takes one of them*. They also agree to forsake all others – in other words to *not have intimate relations with anyone other than their spouse*. Sadly, in our culture today, a large percentage of marriages, even Christian marriages, fail. Why? In many cases, it is because one or both of the persons has broken the covenant. Either they fail to love each other, or they fail to forsake all others. In today's introductory scripture passage, Moses reminds the Israelites not to forget the covenant they had made with God. They had promised to worship and serve no god except the one true God. Marriage is analogous. We promise to love no other person in the intimate way we love our spouse. As we age, let us never break the covenant that we established on our wedding day.

4

Remember to cherish each other and keep the covenant you made to each other as you grow old together.

Discuss Together:
1. Think back to your marriage ceremony. Was the word "covenant" ever discussed or explained to you from a Biblical point of view?
2. **Matthew 19:4-6** records these words of Jesus: "*...he who created them...said, 'Therefore a man shall leave his father and his mother and hold fast to his wife, and the two shall become one flesh'...So they are no longer two but one flesh. What therefore God has joined together, let not man separate.*" In light of this scripture passage, what does the marriage covenant mean to you now?
3. Think back to a time when your marriage covenant was tested, perhaps by temptation, anger, or frustration. Discuss how each of you felt at the time and how you feel about it now.
4. If one or both of you have ever broken the marriage covenant, discuss how that violation made you feel. What did you do (or what *could* you do) to restore your covenant? If not, praise the Lord, and discuss how you have avoided this kind of violation through the years.
5. The gospel is about grace and forgiveness. Forgive each other, just as in Christ, God forgave you. If you need help in this process, please talk to a trusted Christian counselor.

Study Together:
Study **Hebrews 8:1-12**, which describes Jesus Christ as the high priest of a new and better covenant compared to the original covenant God established with the Israelites after he brought them out of slavery in Egypt. The writer quotes **Jeremiah 31**, which points out how the Israelites broke that first covenant, and then he explains how Jesus is the fulfillment of the prophecy about a new covenant. Notice how seriously God takes covenants! Discuss similarities and differences between the covenants of this scripture passage and the marriage covenant. With the Lord's help, you will maintain *your* marriage covenant till death parts you.

Pray Together:
Pray with your spouse for the Lord's help in treasuring and maintaining your marriage covenant.

1. Chores

Growing Old Together...   By John M. Cimbala, 2019

Ethel: I am washing clothes today, so give me any of your light clothes that need to be washed.

Frank: Do you mean light as in not **heavy** or light as in **not dark**? ☺

Ethel: ...☺ ...☹

Artwork by Helen Dickey

God has also given riches and wealth to every man, and He has allowed him to enjoy them, take his reward, and rejoice in his labor. This is a gift of God.
Ecclesiastes 5:19 (HCSB)

Read Together:
Do you complain about having to do chores? The definition of **chore** is "a routine task, especially a household one; regular or daily light work; an unpleasant but necessary task." My natural tendency is to be a complainer, especially with regard to chores. As an example, I often forget to take out the garbage on Thursday nights. My wife usually remembers and says something like, "This is Thursday, dear. Did you remember the Thursday chore that you love to do?" For many years, my typical response was to grunt and complain, "Ugh! I *hate* taking out the garbage!" Then my wife would say, "Be thankful that your arms work and that you can walk and carry out the garbage! Some day you might not be able to, and then you would give anything to take out the garbage!" I would usually grunt again. On reflection, however, my wife's comments were wise and beneficial. As King Solomon instructs us in today's introductory scripture passage, it is a gift of God to be able to work, and we should rejoice in our labor; this includes our unpleasant chores. Over the years, my wife's advice has sunk in, and my attitude about chores has improved. While I cannot claim that I *rejoice* when I take out the garbage, I *can* claim that I no longer grumble and complain about this chore, that

is, *most* of the time. As we age and our strength wanes, once simple chores become more difficult. So, be thankful while you are still able to do chores for each other.

Always watch for opportunities to help your spouse with chores, especially those that become more challenging as you grow old together.

Discuss Together:
1. Discuss some chores performed by your spouse that you greatly appreciate and that you would have a difficult time doing yourself. Thank him or her for regularly doing these and other chores.
2. Are there some chores that you actually *enjoy* doing? Give some reasons why you enjoy these particular chores. Discuss ways to make some of your *other* chores more enjoyable.
3. Mention some chores that are becoming more difficult or even burdensome for you as you age. Discuss practical ways that your spouse can help you with these chores.
4. Discuss practical ways to develop and maintain a positive attitude about your chores, especially those that are somewhat unpleasant. Remind each other (as my wise wife often does) that, as you grow old together, you may reach a point when you are no longer physically able to do those chores and may yearn to be able to do them again.
5. The gospel is about grace and forgiveness. Forgive each other for the times when you have had, shall we say, a "less than thankful" attitude about your chores.

Study Together:
Study **Colossians 3:14-24**, which provides advice from the Apostle Paul about how to live in harmony with other people, to maintain an attitude of thankfulness, and to do all your work as though working for the Lord. Discuss ways to help each other put this advice into practice, especially regarding your chores. With the Lord's help, you will be able to develop a positive attitude about chores. Perhaps you may even learn to *rejoice* in your chores!

Pray Together:
Pray with your spouse for the Lord's help in being thankful for the chores that you are still able to perform.

2. Listening

Growing Old Together...

By John M. Cimbala, 2019

Frank: (annoyed) You are repeating yourself again.
Ethel: That's because you don't *listen*!
Frank: Yes, I *do*...☹
Ethel: Okay, what did I just say to you *two times*?
Frank: Ummm ...I guess I wasn't listening. ...☹
Ethel: ...☺...☹

Artwork by Helen Dickey

Behold, I waited for your words, I listened for your wise sayings, while you searched out what to say.
Job 32:11 (ESV)

Read Together:
Do you *listen* to your spouse? The definition of **listen** is "to give attention with the ear; to attend closely for the purpose of hearing." I am guilty of not always listening closely to my wife and therefore not *hearing*. Sometimes I don't want to be bothered or distracted. Other times I simply don't value my spouse's opinion as I ought. I listen to her first few words and make a quick decision as to whether this is something important or not. If not, I tend to ignore the rest of what she says. Sometimes I even go back to my reading while she is still talking (not recommended, husbands!). Other times my mind wanders off to something "more important." My wife is not easily fooled though. When she knows I am not paying attention to her, she tells me, "Listen with your eyes!" This means making eye contact while the other person is talking. It is hard to be distracted when looking into the eyes of someone who is speaking. My wife is a wise woman, and listening to her with my eyes is the correct response. In today's introductory scripture passage, Elihu, the youngest of Job's friends, vents his frustration. He had waited for Job's friends to give sound advice. He was a good *listener*, and he

undoubtedly listened with his eyes. Unfortunately, after hours of patient listening, he still had not heard anything wise!

Remember to listen to your spouse *with your eyes* as you grow old together. Listen with your heart as well for a more complete understanding of words, both said and unsaid. Then you will never miss his or her words of wisdom.

Discuss Together:
1. Why is it sometimes difficult to really listen to your spouse?
2. Think back to a time when you *did* listen to your spouse, and it turned out to be a wise choice. Discuss.
3. Think back to a time when you *did not* listen to your spouse and were caught in this state of inattentiveness. How did it make you feel? Perhaps more importantly, how do you think it made your spouse feel?
4. What specific steps can you take in order to become a better listener, especially to your spouse?
5. The gospel is about grace and forgiveness. Forgive each other for the times when you have not been a good listener.

Study Together:
Study **Luke 2:41-51**, through which we are given a great example of how to listen – an example from the Lord Jesus Christ himself! Discuss how the young boy Jesus used listening as a tool for learning. With the Lord's help, through practice and patience, you can emulate this example.

Pray Together:
Pray with your spouse and ask for the Lord's help in listening to your spouse not only with open eyes but also with an open heart and an open mind.

3. Flattery

Growing Old Together...

By John M. Cimbala, 2019

Frank: (looking at Ethel) You look exceptionally beautiful today.
Ethel: Uh huh...What do you want?
Frank: Nothing...I just think you look beautiful today.
Ethel: Sure you do...☺
Frank: By the way, do you think you could...
Ethel: ☺

Artwork by Helen Dickey

For we never came with words of flattery, as you know, nor with a pretext for greed—God is witness.
1 Thessalonians 2:5 (ESV)

Read Together:
Have you ever used flattery to try to get something from your spouse? The definition of *flattery* is "excessive, insincere praise or compliment; pandering." Notice the two components of flattery: excessive and insincere. In today's introductory scripture passage, Paul implies that flattery is often given with greedy motives, whereas in his case, he claims God as witness that he never used flattery to achieve his goal of bringing salvation through Christ to the Thessalonian people. Paul knew that flattery gets you nowhere in evangelism. I can testify that it also gets you nowhere in marriage! I know this from experience. I can't get away with flattering my wife. She is able to sense when I am excessive and insincere, and it is usually when either I want something *from* her or I want forgiveness for something I did *to* her. We certainly should compliment our spouses when appropriate. The definition of compliment is "a polite and appropriate expression of praise or admiration." However, excessive and insincere compliments or praise (in other words, *flattery*) is *not* appropriate; nor is it recommended. From a Christian perspective, we should *always* be ready and willing to genuinely love, serve, and forgive

our spouse so that the insincerity of flattery isn't *ever* necessary. It also helps if we remember, as Paul did, that God is witness.

Remember to compliment your spouse often, but don't be like Frank in today's comic. Never use *flattery* for your own greedy advantage as you grow old together.

Discuss Together:
1. What specific attributes turn a compliment into flattery?
2. Think back to a time when you used flattery in order to gain something from your spouse. Why did you feel the need to do so? How do you feel about it now?
3. Discuss what specific steps you can take in your marriage to avoid flattery and the greediness and deception that go along with it.
4. Discuss how to maintain *honesty* during a discussion while at the same time avoiding flattery.
5. The gospel is about grace and forgiveness. Grace and forgiveness provide opportunities for growth; in this instance, growth from insincere expressions to genuine, altruistic expressions. Forgive each other for the times you used flattery for your own selfish advantage.

Study Together:
Study **Daniel 11:31-35**, which shows an extreme example of flattery, namely that of the Antichrist. Discuss how to avoid being deceived. With the Lord's help, you will be one of the wise, rather than the deceived, people mentioned in this passage.

Pray Together:
Pray with your spouse and ask for the Lord's help to avoid being insincere when complimenting your spouse.

4. Aging

Growing Old Together...

By John M. Cimbala, 2019

Frank: (thinking...) What is the first sign of aging?
Ethel: Losing your hair.
Frank: What is the second sign of aging?
Ethel: Your hair turning gray.
Frank: Hmmm...*I am losing my gray hair*! What does *that* mean?
Ethel: ☺
Frank: Why are you looking at me like that?

Artwork by Helen Dickey

So even to old age and gray hairs, O God, do not forsake me, until I proclaim your might to another generation...
Psalm 71:18 (ESV)

Read Together:

Are you afraid of aging? The definition of **aging** is "to grow old; to mature, as wine, cheese, or wood." The second half of that definition may not apply to *people*. While wine, cheese, and wood improve with age, people tend to lose their health, their memory, and their looks. Why do we age? I believe that Adam and Eve were perfect when created by God. If they had not been cursed because of their sin, they would have lived forever. Because of sin and the Fall, however, God introduced the aging process so that Adam would "return to dust." (By the way, even after the curse, Adam lived for 930 years!) I thank God that my wife and I married when we were young and that we are aging at about the same pace; the changes in our bodies have been slow and gradual. Regardless of how old we get, God promises never to forsake us. Likewise, we need to stay committed to our spouse, no matter how old and gray he or she gets. It is our human frailty, our human condition of sinfulness, which causes us to reflect upon and worry about aging as many of us do. Besides, aging shows that we have been blessed with many years here on Earth! In today's introductory scripture passage, David pleads with God

12

not to forsake him even as he grows old and gray. God honored David's prayer, and he will honor *our* prayer as well. He will never forsake us so that we too can proclaim his might to another generation.

Just as God will never forsake you, you need to make a commitment never to forsake your spouse as you grow old together.

Discuss Together:
1. Discuss what would be different in your lives, or what you would do differently, if the aging process suddenly stopped today.
2. Identify a characteristic of the aging process that particularly bothers you. For example, losing your looks, your strength, your memory... Why did you choose this particular characteristic, and why does it bother you so much?
3. Identify a specific way in which you can help your spouse not to get depressed about aging, and in particular the characteristic of aging he or she mentioned in the previous question. You are encouraged to also read or re-read the Flattery devotional as you reflect on this discussion item.
4. Share and reflect on a fun memory from when you were newly married.
5. The gospel is about grace and forgiveness. Pray for forgiveness for the sin of vanity. Forgive each other, and yourself, for times when you have fretted or complained about aging. After all, the process of aging is inevitable and is not in your control.

Study Together:
Study **Genesis 3**, which is the account of the sin of Adam and Eve and what happened as a result. Discuss *why* they disobeyed God's clear command. Pray for wisdom and that God helps you to be obedient to His Word as you grow old together.

Pray Together:
Pray with your spouse and ask for the Lord's help in not forsaking your spouse as you age.

5. Romance

Growing Old Together...

By John M. Cimbala, 2019

Frank: (proudly) Debbie said the novel I wrote is really romantic.

Ethel: Uh huh.

Frank: She said you are lucky to have a sensitive, romantic husband... ☺

Ethel: In real life you are about as sensitive and romantic as a rock.

Frank: ...☹

Artwork by Helen Dickey

When Isaac had been there for some time, Abimelech king of the Philistines looked down from the window and was surprised to see Isaac caressing his wife Rebekah.
Genesis 26:8 (HCSB)

Read Together:

Are you still romantic with your spouse as you grow old together? The definition of ***romantic*** is "displaying or expressing love or strong affection." What strikes me in this definition is the use of the word "love" and the words "strong affection" as if they are interchangeable. *Are* they? Movies and romantic novels emphasize *infatuation* rather than love when portraying the world's view of romance. Two people are attracted to each other physically and so they treat each other "romantically." But this kind of romance is often self-centered – showing romance in order to get something from the other person. In marriage, however, romance should instead emphasize *abiding love*, which goes well beyond infatuation or strong affection and is *other*-centered. To be romantic in a Christian way is to love your spouse even when you are upset about something. Christian romance is much more than mere physical attraction, although such attraction is a God-ordained attribute of his creation of man and woman and is a blessed part of the spousal relationship. In today's introductory scripture passage, the image of Isaac caressing his wife Rebekah is a good example of godly romance. This is especially so if you read these verses in context. At the time, Isaac was trying to deceive Abimelech into thinking that Rebekah was his *sister*, not his wife. But since he could not resist being romantic with his wife, his deception was discovered.

Try to remain romantic (expressing true love) with your spouse as you grow old together.

Discuss Together:
1. Each of you define romance. Then discuss the differences in your definitions.
2. Think back to the time or specific event in your marriage that was the most romantic. Why did you choose that event? What mental images appear in your mind as you recall this event? Take time now to explain to your spouse the meaning and importance of this romantic occurrence.
3. Discuss some of the ways you have demonstrated romance to each other. As you discuss, reflect upon these ways of showing romance. How do they differ, and how are they similar?
4. Discuss some specific ways in which your spouse can be *more* romantic.
5. The gospel is about grace and forgiveness. Forgive each other when you have not been as romantic as you could or should have been.

Study Together:
Study **Genesis 24**, which describes how Abraham arranged for his son Isaac to marry Rebekah and how Isaac responded. How is this an example of romance? With the Lord's help, you will not forget the romance that you had when you were young.

Pray Together:
Pray with your spouse and ask for the Lord's help in being more romantic toward each other.

6. Possessions

Growing Old Together...   By John M. Cimbala, 2019

Frank: I tried your new underarm deodorant. It smells great.
Ethel: Ughh! That's *lip balm*, not underarm deodorant!
Frank: Oh... Sorry.
Ethel: ☹
Frank: Don't worry. I picked out the hairs when I was done.

Artwork by Helen Dickey

Take care, and be on your guard against all covetousness, for one's life does not consist in the abundance of his possessions.
Luke 12:15 (ESV)

Read Together:

Do you treat your spouse's possessions as carefully as you treat your *own* possessions? The definition of **possession** is "having, owning, or controlling something." It strikes me that this definition includes the word *control*. When you own or possess something, you have *control* over that possession and can do with it as you please. When we get married, all our possessions become jointly owned. Even our *bodies* are no longer our own, and we are commanded to share them with our spouse (see 1 Corinthians 7). But does that mean that we have joint control over *everything*? There are some possessions (like toothbrushes and deodorant) that probably should *not* be shared. Likewise, one spouse should avoid trying to *control* the personal possessions of the other spouse. We also need to be sure that we treat our spouse's possessions with respect and care, and we (rightly) expect the same treatment of *our* personal possessions in return. In today's introductory scripture passage, Jesus reminds us that the value of our lives is not proportional to the abundance (or lack) of our possessions. And this is why the first part of that verse exhorts us to guard against covetousness. One good thing about growing old is that, as we gain wisdom, we tend to (or *should* tend to) value personal material possessions less and personal relationships more.

Respect each other's personal possessions as you grow old together.

Discuss Together:
1. Think back to a time when you did not honor one of your spouse's possessions, either accidentally or intentionally. How does it make you feel when you reflect on that incident?
2. Discuss in a mutually respectful way how to come to an understanding as to what is yours, what is your spouse's, and what belongs to both of you.
3. Think of a particular possession your spouse sometimes does not respect. Lovingly explain how this disrespect affects you. Suggest some particular steps he or she can take to show more respect to your possessions.
4. Think about a highly valued worldly possession, and in particular one from before you were married. So that your spouse may understand, explain why this possession holds such significance for you. How hard would it be for you to give it up? What circumstances would need to occur in order for you to give it up willingly?
5. The gospel is about grace and forgiveness. Forgive each other for the times you have not respected each other's possessions.

Study Together:
Study **1 Corinthians 7:1-5**, which discusses how a husband and wife are supposed to relate to each other. Discuss which of these areas need improvement in your own marriage and how to go about such improvement. With the Lord's help, you will be able to follow this model from God's Word.

Pray Together:
Pray with your spouse and ask for the Lord's help in respecting each other's possessions.

7. Intelligence

Growing Old Together...   By John M. Cimbala, 2019

Frank: (looking in the mirror) I am losing *more* gray hair.
Ethel: Uh huh. You're getting old.
Frank: Well, losing my **gray hair** is better than losing my **gray matter**!
Ethel: ☺
Frank: Why are you looking at me like that?
Ethel: ☺

Artwork by Helen Dickey

An intelligent heart acquires knowledge, and the ear of the wise seeks knowledge.
Proverbs 18:15 (ESV)

Read Together:

Are you worried about losing your memory and intelligence as you grow old together? The definition of **intelligence** is "aptitude in grasping truths, relationships, facts, meanings, etc." It is inevitable that our intelligence and aptitude decline as we age. Our brains, along with our bodies, wear out as we get old. Even if we don't have a disease of the mind such as Alzheimer's or dementia, we start to forget things like names, numbers, etc., and cannot think as quickly on our feet. How does this affect our marriage relationship? In my case, as I have observed with other older couples as well, my wife and I have started to complete the other's sentences. Oftentimes one of us is searching for a word that just won't come to mind, but the other one usually knows what we are thinking and provides the word for which we were searching. That is one of the benefits of a long marriage. We often laugh at such forgetfulness. But it would be a lot less humorous if we didn't have a life partner to share these lapses in our intelligence and memory. In today's introductory scripture passage, wise King Solomon encourages us to acquire knowledge. I believe this applies no matter what our age. As humans with an intricate brain, designed and created by an awesome God, we are blessed to be lifelong learners. I have always enjoyed learning and still do. Perhaps an advantage of aging is that, because of our forgetfulness and declining intelligence, we get to learn some things more than once!

Try your best not to become impatient when your spouse forgets things. Instead, stimulate each other's memories as you grow old together.

Discuss Together:
1. What bothers you more as you age: losing some of your looks or losing some of your memory and intelligence? Why?
2. Identify a specific aspect of your spouse's intelligence or an aptitude that you especially appreciate. How does your spouse's intelligence or aptitude complement your own? Discuss why you chose this particular aspect.
3. Identify a specific aspect of *your* intelligence or aptitude that you would especially *not* want to lose. Why is this particular aspect so important to you? How would you cope if major changes to this intelligence or aptitude occurred as you aged?
4. Name a subject or area of knowledge in which you still have a strong desire to learn. Why did you choose this?
5. The gospel is about grace and forgiveness. How will you grant grace to your spouse as age weakens memory?

Study Together:
Study **1 Timothy 4:6-16**, where the Apostle Paul compares physical training to spiritual training and discusses the importance of knowing scripture. Discuss how you, as a couple, can emphasize the spiritual over the physical, even as you age. With the Lord's help, though your physical body inevitably declines, your wisdom and intelligence concerning God's Word will continue to grow.

Pray Together:
Pray with your spouse and ask for the Lord's help, particularly in the items listed by you and by your spouse in Questions 2-4 above.

8. Youthfulness

Growing Old Together...

By John M. Cimbala, 2019

Frank: When I get old and decrepit, are you going to trade me in for a younger model?

Ethel: You're still here, aren't you? ☺

Frank: ...☺ ...☹ Umm...Thanks...I think ...☺.

Ethel: ☺

Artwork by Helen Dickey

The glory of young men is their strength, but the splendor of old men is their gray hair.
Proverbs 20:29 (ESV)

Read Together:

Do you yearn to be young or youthful again? The definition of **youthfulness** is "being in an early stage generally, as of existence, progress, operation, development, or maturity." I suppose all of us in the latter stages of life wouldn't mind having a younger, more attractive *body*. But I wouldn't want to go back to an "earlier stage of maturity" as in the above definition. Sadly, many people discard their aging spouse for a younger, prettier, more handsome, and/or more exciting one, thinking that this will bring happiness and satisfaction. But it rarely does. God's plan for marriage is that we stay together until death claims one of us. It is inevitable that our looks will fade with age, but by God's grace it happens slowly and to both of us simultaneously. Unlike Frank in today's comic, I have no fear that my wife will trade me in for a younger man. Nor should she fear that I will leave her for a younger woman. We have grown spiritually in Christ together over almost four decades. At this point younger models shouldn't even be a temptation for us. Besides, youthful people are by definition immature, and there are many advantages to having an older, more mature spouse. Today's introductory scripture passage reminds us that gray hair in an older man (or woman) can be splendorous, even as he or she loses physical strength and attractiveness.

Learn to appreciate your spouse for qualities that do not depend on youthfulness, especially physical attractiveness, as you grow old together.

Discuss Together:

1. What aspect(s) of being young and youthful do you *miss* the most? Why?
2. What aspect(s) of maturing and growing old together do you *appreciate* the most? Why?
3. Compliment your spouse about something you appreciate that he or she does – something totally unrelated to physical appearance.
4. Is there an area in which you have sometimes felt unappreciated by your spouse? Discuss how being unappreciated makes you feel, and then together discuss some specific ways in which this lack of appreciation can be remedied.
5. The gospel is about grace and forgiveness. Forgive each other, especially for the item(s) mentioned in Question 4 above.

Study Together:

Study **Titus 2**, in which the Apostle Paul urges older men and women to be examples to those who are younger and thereby train them to live godly lives. Discuss how your maturity can be used in this same way to train younger people in their spiritual walk, and pray for the Lord's help.

Pray Together:

Pray with your spouse, and ask for the Lord's help in appreciating each other for things that really matter, not just for how you both look.

9. Forgetfulness

Growing Old Together... <small>By John M. Cimbala, 2019</small>

Frank: You're starting to forget things.
Ethel: So are you.
Frank: No I'm not. I can't even remember the last time I forgot anything! ☺
Ethel: ☹

Artwork by Helen Dickey

I will delight in your statutes; I will not forget your word.
Psalm 119:16 (ESV)

Read Together:
Is your spouse getting more forgetful as you grow old together? Are *you*? The definition of ***forget*** is "to omit or neglect unintentionally." It is easy to be critical of one's spouse when he or she forgets something – especially something important that leads to an inconvenience or costs extra money. But we should highlight the word *unintentionally* in the above definition of forget. As peoples' minds get forgetful with age, we need to remember that they are not forgetting intentionally or with evil intent. Our minds wear out with age just like our bodies do, so we find it harder to remember things as we grow older. In most cases it happens to both the husband and the wife, and we need to learn to help each other remember. It is most difficult when *your* spouse is the forgetful one, especially if he or she develops some form of dementia. In today's introductory scripture passage, David prays that he will not forget God's word. I often pray the same prayer since I memorize large portions of scripture (e.g., whole chapters and books of the Bible). I have shared with my family that, even if I lose much of my memory as I age, I pray that, like David, I will not forget the word of God. There is *one* kind of forgetfulness, however, for which we can be thankful: God says in **Isaiah 43:25**, "*I am he who blots out your transgressions for my own sake, and I*

22

will not remember your sins." I am glad that God forgets our sins when we repent and trust in the Lord Jesus Christ as the substitutionary sacrifice for our sins.

Don't forget to forgive and forget as you grow old together.

Discuss Together:
1. Think back to a time when you forgot something important in your marriage (anniversary, appointment, …). What was your spouse's reaction? Hopefully you can look back at that incident and laugh with each other.
2. Identify a specific, recurring act of forgetfulness on the part of your spouse that particularly frustrates you. Brainstorm ways to help avoid repeating this specific act in the future.
3. Is there a certain area in which you feel that *your* memory is waning? If so, discuss possible reminders or specific actions you and/or your spouse can take to help each other.
4. Each of you list the top five things that you do *not* want to forget as you grow old and forgetful.
5. The gospel is about grace and forgiveness. Forgive each other for your forgetfulness, and pray for each other. Always remember that it is through Christ that God forgives you.

Study Together:
Study **2 Timothy 2:1-13**, in which the Apostle Paul gives advice to his young, and sometimes timid, son in the faith, Timothy. Notice and discuss what Paul reminds Timothy not to forget. With the Lord's help, you also will not forget this.

Pray Together:
Pray with your spouse and ask for the Lord's help as you grow older and more forgetful. In particular, pray for the items listed in Question 4 above. If the following item did not make your list, pray that you do not forget that Jesus Christ is our Savior and Redeemer.

10. Hearing

Growing Old Together...

By John M. Cimbala, 2019

Frank: (walking closer) I think you're going deaf. I yelled three times, asking you what's for dinner.

Ethel: (irritated) And I answered you three times: Lasagna. Lasagna. Lasagna!

Frank: Oh...I guess I wasn't paying attention.

Ethel: ☹

Artwork by Helen Dickey

This is why I speak to them in parables, because seeing they do not see, and hearing they do not hear, nor do they understand. ...the prophecy of Isaiah is fulfilled that says: "You will indeed hear but never understand, and you will indeed see but never perceive."
Matthew 13:13-14 (ESV)

Read Together:
Are you getting hard of hearing as you grow old together? The definition of ***hearing*** is "to listen to; give or pay attention to." I like this definition because it involves more than just the mere physical process of perceiving sound with our ears. There is a huge difference between hearing and *listening*. Even more importantly, the above definition stresses that real hearing also involves paying attention to what is being said. That is where I often fail. I hear my wife talk, but I often don't listen or pay attention to what she is saying. As I ponder why, I realize that it is my sinful human condition of pure selfishness that leads me to not listen. I would rather not be bothered by her concerns. I would rather keep doing what I am doing to please myself than to give of myself to listen to her needs. Sure, I admit that my hearing is not as sharp as it was in my youth, but I can still hear my wife when she speaks to me. It is in the *listening* **and** in the *paying attention* where I often fail. I need to learn to pay close attention to what my spouse is saying (and I am sure many of you do, too). We must try, as equipped by the Holy Spirit, to not be like

24

the people whom Jesus chastises in today's introductory scripture passage: who hear but do not *understand*, who see but do not *perceive*.

Make sure you really *hear* each other (translation: *pay attention*) as you grow old together.

Discuss Together:
1. Why is inattentiveness a sign of selfishness? Can you think of a specific example?
2. Reflect upon an event in which you were like the Jewish religious leaders of Jesus day, who heard but did not understand or pay attention. How do you think your spouse felt about this? As you talk about this, offer an apology to your spouse.
3. List some specific ideas that could help *you* to become a better listener.
4. Without being too critical, discuss one or more specific ways that could help your *spouse* to be a better listener.
5. The gospel is about grace and forgiveness. Forgive each other for not listening to each other as attentively as you should.

Study Together:
Study **John 18:33-40**, the famous exchange between Jesus Christ and Pilate the governor. Pay special attention to what the Lord tells Pilate about listening to him, and discuss Pilate's response. With the Lord's help, you, *unlike* Pilate, will listen to the voice of the Lord.

Pray Together:
Pray with your spouse and ask for the Lord's help in being less selfish and a better listener.

11. Planning

Growing Old Together...

By John M. Cimbala, 2019

Frank: (irritated) Why do *you* keep telling *me* what to do? You're not my boss!
Ethel: I don't tell you what to do. I just help you plan your day. ☺
Frank: Oh. ...☺ ...

Artwork by Helen Dickey

The plans of the diligent lead surely to abundance, but everyone who is hasty comes only to poverty.
Proverbs 21:5 (ESV)

Read Together:

Do you need help planning your daily activities as you grow old together? The definition of ***planning*** is "designing and arranging, in advance, details for future benefits or needs." It is wise to plan ahead, not just for the long-term but also for each *day*. As we age and become more forgetful, we need to come up with ways to remember what we need to accomplish on a given day. Many from my generation make lists on paper to carry around with them. Other more tech-savvy people use a reminder app on their cellphones to ensure they don't forget something. But many of us often ignore or neglect to tap into perhaps the best aid for planning our day with which the Lord has blessed us: our *spouse*! My wife makes lists of things she wants me to do – my "honey do" list. Sometimes I don't appreciate such lists. I have my own agenda and selfish desires for my day that often leave little room for what *she* wants me to do. Yet as I think back on our years together, *her* lists of requests have usually been more important and necessary than my own selfish lists of activities. Husband and wife, together, need to generate these "honey do" lists because, as Solomon reminds us in today's introductory scripture passage, the plans of the diligent lead surely to abundance; but neglect of planning may lead to poverty. I don't think Solomon was limiting this advice to merely *financial* abundance or poverty. His advice applies *spiritually* as well.

Don't be too proud to work hand in hand, literally and figuratively, with your spouse to plan your day(s) as you grow old together.

Discuss Together:
1. Both of you answer this question in turn: Are you a planner, or do you prefer to "go with the flow?" Then discuss whether you agree with your spouse's answer or not, and why. Discuss how any differences or similarities in planning styles complement each other and enrich the relationship.
2. Think of some activity or chore that you are finding more difficult as you age and for which better planning might be helpful. Discuss it with your spouse and determine some ways to better plan this activity.
3. Repeat the above, except choose an activity or chore that you noticed may be a potential problem for your *spouse*. Discuss.
4. Do you dislike when your spouse tries to plan your day for you? Why? Discuss ways you can help each other without coming across as bossy.
5. The gospel is about grace and forgiveness. Forgive each other when you haven't followed through with a mutually agreed upon plan. Also forgive your spouse for not always accepting your planning eagerly and without complaining.

Study Together:
Study **2 Chronicles 7:11-22**, which describes how King Solomon successfully accomplished the careful plans he had made to build the great Temple of God and how he was commended for it. Note and discuss the warnings at the end of the chapter. With the Lord's help, you will never abandon the most important planning of your life, namely, your plans to worship the One True God.

Pray Together:
Pray with your spouse and ask for the Lord's help as you assist each other in planning your days, weeks, months, and years.

12. Perfectionism

Growing Old Together...   By John M. Cimbala, 2019

Ethel: Am I a perfectionist?
Frank: Well, you married *me*,
         didn't you? ☺
Ethel: Yes. I guess that settles it.
Frank: Yup. ☺ ...☹ ...
         Wait... That settles it
         which way?
Ethel: ☺

Artwork by Helen Dickey

But he said to me, "My grace is sufficient for you, for my power is made perfect in weakness. Therefore I will boast all the more gladly of my weaknesses, so that the power of Christ may rest upon me."
2 Corinthians 12:9 (ESV)

Read Together:
As you grow old together, do you find yourself becoming more of a perfectionist? The definition of **perfectionist** is "a person who refuses to accept any standard short of perfection." The problem with perfectionism is that nothing in this life is perfect, no matter how hard we wish it were. If you cannot accept any "standard short of perfection," you are in for some huge disappointments in life, including in your marriage. No spouse is perfect, although someone else's spouse may *appear* that way sometimes (but only on the surface). As we grow older, our imperfections become more prominent, often irritating our spouse who has to cope with them. What can we do to avoid judging each other's imperfections? We can start with today's introductory scripture passage. Paul tells us that God's grace is sufficient. He also explains that God's power is made perfect in *weakness*. What does he mean? How can our *weakness* lead to *perfection*? I think the answer is that it forces us to rely on God and on God alone. The weaker we get, the more we need power from above, and that power is perfect power. It is similar in marriage. The weaker and more imperfect we get as we grow old, the more we need to rely on each other and on the Lord to strengthen and help us.

Stop criticizing your spouse's imperfections as you grow old together. Remember that God's power is made perfect in our weakness.

Discuss Together:
1. Does it frustrate or anger you when your spouse does not meet *your* standard of perfection? Why? What steps can you and/or your spouse take to avoid this frustration?
2. Think of something specific that your spouse has done (preferably something recurring) that you feel is not up to your standard of perfection – something that bothers you but that you may not have addressed. Gently discuss ways he or she can improve in this area. Conversely, discuss ways your spouse can assist you in accepting this "imperfection" or relaxing your own standard of perfection in this area.
3. Think of something that your spouse does that *is* perfect (or nearly so), and tell him or her how much you appreciate it. Offer a contrite apology for the times you have failed to show appreciation for this "perfect" action.
4. Discuss a time in your life when you felt weak or helpless and had to rely on God and others to get through it. Did you feel any *power* in your weakness as God's grace embraced you? If God's grace during this time of weakness was exemplified by your spouse, share that, and thank him or her. If that ultimate grace was showered upon you by another, make an opportunity to express your thankfulness.
5. The gospel is about grace and forgiveness. Forgive each other for the times you have unfairly demanded perfection from your spouse.

Study Together:
Study **2 Corinthians 11:30-12:10**, in which Paul does a little boasting while emphasizing his weaknesses. Discuss how his weaknesses made him stronger in the Lord. With the Lord's help, the same will be true of you.

Pray Together:
Pray with your spouse and ask for the Lord's help not only in accepting each other's weaknesses and imperfections but also in relishing each other's fallible human characteristics as an avenue of grace. Reaffirm your vow to help each other as much as possible.

13. Anger

Growing Old Together...   By John M. Cimbala, 2019

Ethel: Are you still angry at me?
Frank: I guess so.
Ethel: What do you mean, you **guess** so?
Frank: ...☺ ... Well, I forgot *why* I was angry at you in the first place.
Ethel: Getting old has its advantages. ☺

Artwork by Helen Dickey

Be angry and do not sin; do not let the sun go down on your anger.
Ephesians 4:26 (ESV)

Read Together:

All of us occasionally get angry at our spouses. But has your anger intensified or become more frequent as you grow old together? If so, you need to discern *why* and then discuss with your spouse ways to ameliorate that anger. The definition of ***anger*** is "a strong feeling of annoyance, displeasure, or hostility." I trust there is no hostility in your marriage, but annoyance and displeasure – now *these* are huge contributors to anger. They certainly are for *me*. When my wife keeps talking on and on about something that does not interest me, I get annoyed. When she does something or makes *me* do something that takes me away from what I really *want* to do, I become displeasured with her. I can endure only so much annoyance and displeasure before it turns to anger. This is *selfish* anger, not *righteous* anger. In today's introductory scripture passage, Paul tells us to be angry, so we assume that this refers to righteous anger. This kind of anger is against injustice, against sin, against anything that does not agree with the way God wants and instructs us to act. He continues: "...*and* (some translations use the word *but*) do not sin." We assume that the kind of sinful anger Paul refers to here is *selfish* anger. For example, anger at our spouse because of annoyance or displeasure does not qualify as righteous; rather, it is a result of our sinful human condition. When such anger is stirred, we need

30

to make a conscious effort to stop it so as to avoid this sinful, rather than righteous, anger. And we need to do so before we go to bed, as Paul also commands.

Life is too short to spend it in anger. When you get annoyed with your spouse to the point of anger, recognize your sinful emotion, communicate about it with your spouse, offer a sincere apology, and move on. Be quick to forgive as you grow old together.

Discuss Together:
1. Think back to an incident in which anger toward your spouse was stronger than necessary. What precipitated this intense feeling? How did you feel later, after you calmed down? If you neglected to do so at the time, apologize now to your spouse for this occurrence.
2. Consider again the incident of the previous question. Discuss what you could perhaps have done to prevent the anger and/or the actions the anger initiated.
3. Discuss some concrete and specific steps you can learn and implement as a couple to avoid the unproductivity and hurt of getting angry with each other.
4. Do you express the kind of anger commanded by God in today's introductory scripture passage verse? In what type of incidences would such "righteous anger" be acceptable? Discuss other types of incidents during which the idea of righteous anger may be abused/misused.
5. The gospel is about grace and forgiveness. Forgive each other for the times you have lashed out in anger at your spouse.

Study Together:
Study **Jonah 4**, which describes Jonah's anger after God relented from destroying Nineveh. Discuss why Jonah reacted this way and how God responded to Jonah's anger. With the Lord's help, you will not be like Jonah.

Pray Together:
Pray with your spouse and ask for the Lord's help in developing self control over any angry impulses. Ask for an additional measure of Holy Spirit in these matters.

14. Tiredness

Laugh Together:

Growing Old Together...   By John M. Cimbala, 2019

Ethel: (exhausted) I'm so tired, I feel like I'm going to collapse.

Frank: Can you wait till after you make dinner? I'm hungry.

Ethel: ☹

Frank: Just kidding! JK ! ...JK !

Ethel: ☹

Frank: Women have no sense of humor.

Artwork by Helen Dickey

They have sown wheat and have reaped thorns; they have tired themselves out but profit nothing.
Jeremiah 12:13 (ESV)

Read Together:

Do you *tire* more easily as you are growing old together? I certainly do, and so does my wife. Tiredness is one of the attributes of aging. Our bodies and minds lack the stamina that we had in our youth. The definition of **tired** is "exhausted, as by exertion; fatigued or sleepy; in need of rest; weary." Yes, these definitions hit the nail on the head, as the saying goes. Sometimes in the evening I feel *all* of the conditions listed above (exhaustion, fatigue, sleepiness, weariness) at the very time when I know I should read my Bible, work on my Sunday school lesson, take care of neglected chores around the house... Tiredness leads to a lack of motivation to do any of these things. It is much easier to plop in front of the TV and watch the news or some banal show. I think we can all relate to today's introductory scripture passage; sometimes we work diligently (sow wheat) but achieve nothing, or even worse than nothing, in return (reap thorns). Oftentimes we have tired ourselves out by the daily grind of life, yet it seems like we *profit* nothing. At times like these, it is good to remember what our Lord Jesus Christ said, *"Come to me, all who labor and are heavy laden, and I will give you rest."* Only that kind of rest can ultimately cure our tiredness.

When your spouse is exhausted or discouraged, try doing something *for* him or her – something that he or she normally does but lacks the motivation due to tiredness. Such unselfish acts of kindness help *both* of you cope with tiredness as you grow old together.

Discuss Together:
1. Think upon a time when you were *really* exhausted. What circumstances led to this? How could you perhaps have avoided excessive tiredness in that particular situation?
2. Think of one of your chores (daily or weekly) that often leads you toward exhaustion, especially as you are growing older. What is your attitude when this happens? If your attitude is somewhat negative, discuss *positive* ways to improve it.
3. Discuss practical ways in which you can help your spouse when he or she is really tired. In particular, use the item from the previous question.
4. In your Christian walk, do you feel like you receive *rest* when you come to the Lord as you labor and are heavy laden? Why or why not? Can you give an example?
5. The gospel is about grace and forgiveness. Forgive your spouse for a time when he or she did not meet your expectations due to exhaustion.

Study Together:
Study **1 Samuel 30:1-25**, which describes how two hundred of David's men had given all that they could give and were too exhausted to fight. Discuss how David treated these men. Contrast this with how some of the men who *did* fight treated them. With the Lord's help, you can show similar kindness to others, especially your *spouse*, when he or she is weary and doesn't do what you expect.

Pray Together:
Pray with your spouse and ask for the Lord's help in scheduling your time so that you don't get exhausted.

15. Sickness

Laugh Together:

Growing Old Together...   By John M. Cimbala, 2019

Frank: (distressed) I keep getting headaches.
Ethel: Maybe you need to get a CAT scan of your brain.
Frank: They won't find anything.
Ethel: ☺ ... That's for sure... ☺
Frank: ...☺ ...Maybe women *do* have a sense of humor after all.
Ethel: ☺

Artwork by Helen Dickey

A man's spirit will endure sickness, but a crushed spirit who can bear?
Proverbs 18:14 (ESV)

Read Together:

Although I am continually grateful for the gift of my wife, I am most thankful for her when I am feeling unwell. There are times in life (and such times occur more frequently as we grow old together) when an illness, some kind of sickness, or even a bad headache attacks our aging bodies and makes us miserable. It is an undeserved blessing to have a spouse to comfort and care for us during these times of sickness. The definition of **sickness** is "ill health; a disordered, weakened, or unsound condition." Of these descriptions the word "weakened" stands out to me. When I get sick, I lose the strength and stamina to function normally; I get weak. In times of illness, I appreciate the care my wife provides for me, like bringing me something to eat, finding the right medicine, or doing a chore that I normally would do but lack the stamina at that moment. Her loving attentiveness lifts my spirit and, as Solomon says in today's introductory scripture passage, enables me to endure sickness. I try to return the favor when *she* is the one not feeling well, but I must admit that I lack somewhat in empathy compared to her. In times of sickness, it is good to remember our wedding vows, "...to have and to hold, from this day forward, for better, for worse, for richer, for poorer, in sickness and in health, to love and to cherish till death do us part...."

Sickness is an inevitable part of life because of Adam's sin. But even in sickness we can show the love of Christ to others, especially to our spouse.

Whether in sickness or in health, always be sensitive to your spouse's needs as you grow old together.

Discuss Together:
1. Reflect upon a time you were ill. How did your spouse show empathy and help you? Express gratitude to him or her for these acts of kindness.
2. Some people say that you grow more through difficult times than easy times. Have you found this to be true when you have gone through an illness? Discuss why or why not.
3. Think about a couple in which either the husband or the wife needed to take care of the other in a time of terrible illness, perhaps one that led eventually to death. What did you appreciate about them, and what can you learn from them?
4. Renew your marriage vows about loving each other through better or worse, etc., especially through sickness and health. Reassure your spouse that you will be there for him or her if such times of illness come.
5. The gospel is about grace and forgiveness. Forgive each other for times when you were not suitably sensitive to your spouse's needs during an illness.

Study Together:
Study **2 Corinthians 12:1-10**, where the Apostle Paul writes, "When I am weak, then I am strong." Discuss what Paul meant by that statement. When in your Christian walk have you found this to be true for you? With the Lord's help, you and your spouse will always be willing to assist and strengthen each other in your weaknesses.

Pray Together:
Pray with your spouse and ask for the Lord's help as you strengthen and assist each other in times of sickness and weakness.

16. Fragrance

Growing Old Together...

By John M. Cimbala, 2019

Frank: (sniffing) Why do you smell so good?

Ethel: Because I don't have hair on every square inch of my body.

Frank: ☺ ...☺ ... Wait... Are you saying that *I don't* smell good?

Ethel: Don't ask so many questions.

Frank: ...☺ ...

Artwork by Helen Dickey

Your lips drip nectar, my bride; honey and milk are under your tongue; the fragrance of your garments is like the fragrance of Lebanon.
Song of Solomon 4:11 (ESV)

Read Together:

Do you enjoy the fragrance of your spouse? The definition of *fragrance* is "a pleasant aroma; a sweet or pleasing scent or smell." My wife's fragrance certainly meets this definition. I am not talking about her perfume; I mean the smell of her *skin* – it just smells good to me! I've read that each of us has a unique scent due to our body chemistry, especially, and perhaps surprisingly, because of the aromatic by-products of our *immune* system. Of course, good hygiene is also critical to smelling good. In animal scents, pheromones are known to be important; however, the studies are inconclusive about the role of pheromones in human beings. Regardless of the *cause* of our fragrance, it seems to play a part in our initial attraction to each other. As we grow old together, we get used to each other's fragrance; after many years together, the fragrance of our spouse is also a source of *comfort*. Sometimes when I hug my wife, I like to just slowly breathe in the fragrant smell of her neck. It seems that Solomon also enjoyed his wife's fragrance – even after it was absorbed into her *clothing*, as we see in today's introductory scripture passage. In Ephesians 5:2, Paul says *"Christ loved us and gave himself up for us, a fragrant offering and sacrifice to God."* Paul is implying here that the sacrifice Christ made for us was pleasing (a pleasant aroma) in the sight of God. This undeserved gift, this offering of self, draws us to God just as the fragrance of our spouse draws the two of us together.

As you grow old together, enjoy the sweet fragrance of your spouse.

Discuss Together:
1. Perhaps you have never thought about this previously, but how would you describe the fragrance of your spouse?
2. The Apostle Paul tells us that Christ's love and sacrifice was a fragrant offering to God. List some ways in which your love and sacrifice for your spouse can be a fragrant offering to God.
3. Wrap your arms around your spouse, and breathe deeply. Drink in the fragrance. Notice the subtle reactions of your body and mind as you breathe. How does the scent of your spouse cause you to feel?
4. Scientists tell us that fragrances (certain foods, perfumes, the smell of the sea, ...) can trigger vivid memories. Can you think of such a fragrance? What memory does it trigger? Discuss how it makes you feel.
5. The gospel is about grace and forgiveness. Forgive each other for times when you took the fragrance of your spouse's love for granted.

Study Together:
Study **2 Corinthians 2:14-17**, which discusses how we as Christians are an aroma or fragrance of Christ. Discuss this passage and what it means to you. With the Lord's help, you can be a fragrance of Christ toward your spouse and others.

Pray Together:
Pray with your spouse and thank the Lord for giving you the sense of smell. Thank Him for the fragrance of your spouse.

17. Aroma

Growing Old Together...

By John M. Cimbala, 2019

Frank: Do I smell good?
Ethel: It depends on what you compare to.
Frank: ...☺ ...What do you mean? Give me an example.
Ethel: I grew up on a farm, so compared to *that*, you smell **very good**! ☺
Frank: ...☺ ...

Artwork by Helen Dickey

But the firstborn of a cow, ... sheep, or ... goat, you shall not redeem; they are holy. You shall sprinkle their blood on the altar and shall burn their fat as a food offering, with a pleasing aroma to the LORD.
Numbers 18:17 (ESV)

Read Together:

Are you a pleasing aroma to your spouse? The definition of **aroma** is "a distinctive, typically pleasant smell or fragrance; an agreeable odor." In a previous devotional, I talked about my wife's fragrance or aroma. I would rather not talk about *my* aroma, which is not nearly as pleasant as my wife's, especially when I sweat. But aroma has more significance than simply a pleasant smell. There is aroma in how we present ourselves to others, our overall appeal or attractiveness. In marriage our spouse is a pleasing aroma to us, and in turn, we to our spouse. That aroma is an often unrecognized but significant component of the marital relationship. Did you know that *God* enjoys aromas? When we read the Old Testament books of Exodus, Leviticus, and Numbers, we find numerous passages that describe how the ascending smoke of burnt sacrifices was received as a pleasing aroma to the Lord. In today's introductory scripture passage we are told that the burnt offering of a firstborn animal was an especially pleasing aroma to the Lord. We no longer need to offer burnt sacrifices because Jesus Christ, the ultimate firstborn son, was sacrificed for us once and for all. In turn, we are to be the aroma of Christ to others. Paul says in **2 Corinthians 2:15**, "*For we* [Christians] *are the aroma of Christ to God among those who are being saved and among those who are perishing.*"

As you grow old together, make sure that you are the aroma of Christ to God, to your spouse, and to others.

Discuss Together:
1. Think about the Old Testament sacrificial system and why such sacrifices were a pleasing aroma to God. Discuss how the sacrifice of Jesus Christ was an infinitely *more* pleasing aroma.
2. The word "aroma" may not be part of our everyday vocabulary. What does the Apostle Paul mean when he says that we are the "aroma of Christ?"
3. Discuss some specific ways in which you can be an "aroma of Christ" to your spouse.
4. Discuss some specific ways in which you and your spouse (together) can be an "aroma of Christ" to other people.
5. The gospel is about grace and forgiveness. Discuss how forgiveness is a key component of being an "aroma of Christ" to your spouse.

Study Together:
Study **Revelation 5:6-8, 8:1-5**, where the Apostle John makes an analogy between the aroma of burning incense to the prayers of the saints. Discuss why John uses this analogy, particularly in light of the Old Testament passages about the pleasing aroma of animal sacrifices and the New Testament passages about the pleasing aroma of Christ's sacrifice. With the Lord's help, your prayers will be like the aroma of incense to God.

Pray Together:
Pray with your spouse and ask for the Lord's help in being an aroma of Christ to each other and to other people.

18. Attractiveness

Growing Old Together...

By John M. Cimbala, 2019

Frank: (looking in mirror) Am I hot?

Ethel: You have a high metabolism, and so... *yes* you *are* hot.

Frank: ☺ ...No, I mean the *other* kind of hot.

Ethel: At our age, hotness doesn't matter anymore. ☺

Frank: You didn't answer my question...☺ ...

Artwork by Helen Dickey

Then his father and his mother said to him, "... you go to take a wife from the uncircumcised Philistines?" But Samson said to his father, "Get her for me, for she looks good to me."
Judges 14:3 (NASB)

Read Together:

How important is physical *attractiveness* in a marriage, in particular as we grow old together? The definition of **attractiveness** is "providing pleasure or delight, especially in appearance; the quality of being appealing to the senses." Men are often more affected by a woman's appearance than vice-versa, especially when young. Today's introductory scripture passage tells us that when Samson was young, he was attracted to a Philistine woman, not because of her character, but because she "looked good" to him. I certainly do not claim Samson as any kind of role model, but I admit that the initial attraction to the young woman who would later become my wife was physical; she was cute and had a sweet smile. But as we started to know each other better, other aspects of her character became more important than her outward beauty – loyalty, godliness, honesty, integrity... A long-lasting marriage cannot be based on physical attractiveness alone. It is inevitable that our appearance will change with age. We get wrinkles, gain weight, lose hair. But our *character* should *grow* with age, especially when we put Jesus Christ at the center of our marriage.

Try to stay as physically attractive as you are able. But more importantly, strive to improve the attractiveness of your spirit and character as you grow old together.

Discuss Together:
1. Recollect when you first met your spouse. What quality or attribute of him or her was the most attractive to you? Why?
2. What qualities of your spouse are most appealing to you *now*? Are they the same as those of the previous question? Why or why not?
3. Discuss the differences between how men and women define attractiveness in the opposite sex. Do these differences appeal to you, or do they sometimes frustrate you? Discuss.
4. What aspect of the inevitable alteration of your physical attractiveness, due to aging, bothers you the most? Why? Assure your spouse that his or her physical attractiveness is not the most important kind of attractiveness. Remind him or her of the quality you picked in Question 2 above.
5. The gospel is about grace and forgiveness. Forgive each other for the times you may have been harsh with your spouse. Encourage each other to be attractive in ways that matter most to you, personally, as a couple. Encourage each other to be attractive in the eyes of God, as well.

Study Together:
Study **Judges 14**, which tells the account of Samson's marriage to a Philistine woman and the repercussions. Discuss how Samson let physical attractiveness and lust destroy his marriage. Thank the Lord that your marriage is not based on physical attractiveness alone. With the Lord's help, other qualities will attract you even closer to your spouse.

Pray Together:
Pray with your spouse and ask for the Lord's help in appreciating *all* the attractive qualities of your spouse, especially those qualities that are richer and deeper than mere physical attractiveness.

19. Cleanliness

Growing Old Together...

By John M. Cimbala, 2019

Frank: I found a really big dust bunny under our bed.
Ethel: Uh huh...The sweeper doesn't reach way under there. Where did you put it?
Frank: Put it?
Ethel: ☹

Artwork by Helen Dickey

You blind Pharisee! First clean the inside of the cup and the plate, that the outside also may be clean.
Matthew 23:26 (ESV)

Read Together:

In many marriages one person (usually the wife) strives for cleanliness in the house, while the other one (usually the husband) is more lax about keeping the house clean. This can lead to strife not only in a new marriage, but also in a mature marriage as you grow old together. The definition of **cleanliness** is "the state or quality of being clean; being careful to keep clean." I teach the second law of thermodynamics in my college classes. In simple terms, the second law says that everything naturally tends to wind down, to get worse, to go toward a state of disrepair or disorder. I often use a house as an example. If we don't clean our house, it gets dirty all by itself. Dust, skin flakes, dirt dragged in from the yard, food that fell from the table... all of these things make our house dirty without any effort. But it takes effort to clean it! A dirty house cannot clean itself – that would violate the second law of thermodynamics! I am thankful that my wife cleans our house regularly even though I am somewhat more tolerant of dirt. In today's introductory scripture passage, Jesus chastises the Pharisees for cleaning the outsides of the cups while leaving the insides dirty. He explains what he really means two verses later, *"So you also outwardly appear righteous to* *others, but within you are full of hypocrisy and lawlessness.*" We need to remember that cleanliness on the *inside* is even more important than cleanliness on the *outside*.

Strive for cleanliness as you grow old together, not only in your home and in your outward appearance, but also in your heart.

Discuss Together:
1. Think of one or two specific cleaning activities that your spouse does and that you appreciate. Express your sincere appreciation to him or her.
2. Think of something that your spouse does that causes *un*cleanliness, perhaps something that you have not mentioned to him or her, but that bothers you. Gently explain to your spouse *why* it bothers you. Then together discuss concrete ways in which this activity, or habit, can be improved.
3. Is there a cleaning activity which you have taken responsibility for by "default" but which you would be much happier if your spouse did? Discuss it with your spouse, and together think of possible remedies. If you both agree, commit to one of the remedies. Perhaps a "trade" of chores will solve the issue?
4. Have you ever done something that made you feel dirty on the inside even though you appeared clean on the outside? If you have not already done so, confess this sin to our Lord and Savior who has already guaranteed you complete forgiveness. Then, confess this to your spouse and ask for forgiveness.
5. The gospel is about grace and forgiveness. Forgive each other for the times when you may not have exhibited as much cleanliness as you should have, both on the outside and more importantly on the inside.

Study Together:
Study **Psalm 51**, David's well-known psalm about cleansing and forgiveness, which he wrote after his sin with Bathsheba. Discuss what it means to be cleansed from sin. Pray for cleansing of your own sins.

Pray Together:
Pray with your spouse and ask for the Lord's help in maintaining cleanliness on the inside as well as on the outside.

20. Compassion

Growing Old Together...   By John M. Cimbala, 2019

Ethel: Why don't you ever ask me how I am feeling?
Frank: I don't know. I guess I never think about it.
Ethel: ......
Frank: So...How are you feeling?
Ethel: Don't ask.
Frank: ☺

Artwork by Helen Dickey

Put on then, as God's chosen ones, holy and beloved, compassionate hearts, kindness, humility, meekness, and patience.
Colossians 3:12 (ESV)

Read Together:

Are you inherently compassionate, or is compassion not one of your natural gifts? The definition of **compassion** is "sympathetic concern for the sufferings or misfortunes of others; empathy." While I am *concerned* when others suffer, I don't have the natural tendency to want to *do* something about it. When someone is hurting, however, my wife is quick to call, visit, take over a meal... whatever might help the other person. Scientific research has proven that women are, indeed, more empathetic than are men. When someone is in need, men are wired to solve the problem and then move on, but women are wired to empathize, show compassion, give a hug, cry with the hurting person, talk it out. In today's introductory scripture passage Paul reminds us that, as Christians (God's chosen ones), we need to have compassionate hearts. Husbands, it may not come naturally for you, but your wife sometimes needs you to just sit quietly and listen to how she feels and show some empathy for her struggles, rather than simply telling her how to solve the problem. And wives, be patient with your husbands who often don't even have a clue that something is wrong. This is an area in which men and women were created differently, and we need to recognize and accept our differences in order to avoid conflict and hard feelings.

As you grow old together, strive to pay closer attention to how your spouse is feeling and to show compassion and empathy, even if it doesn't come naturally to you.

Discuss Together:

1. Are you naturally compassionate, or do compassion and empathy come with difficulty for you? Think together of ways that you can improve in this area.
2. Encourage your spouse by reminding (and thanking) him or her about a time when he or she showed you compassion, especially unexpected (perhaps *undeserved*) compassion.
3. Inform your spouse about a specific item in which you would appreciate a little more compassion. Then together discuss concrete ways for him or her to first *recognize* your need and then to *follow through* with compassion and empathy.
4. Think of other couples, perhaps in your family or church, who have demonstrated compassion toward each other. What specific attributes of their compassion can you try to emulate? How?
5. The gospel is about grace and forgiveness. Forgive each other for not always being as compassionate as you should. Pray for help in this area in the future.

Study Together:

Study **Isaiah 49:8-18**, which discusses God's compassion for his people. Discuss how the compassion of God is clearly demonstrated in this passage. With the Lord's help, you will be compassionate toward other people just as God is compassionate toward you.

Pray Together:

Pray with your spouse and ask for the Lord's help in being compassionate toward other people, especially toward your life partner.

21. Differences

Growing Old Together...

By John M. Cimbala, 2019

Frank: (romantically) Do I still drive you crazy? ♥
Ethel: Yes, you certainly do.
Frank: ♥...☺
Ethel: But in a different way than when we were young.
Frank: ☺... Wait...☹ ...What do you mean by *different*?
Ethel: ☺

Artwork by Helen Dickey

Jesus Christ is the same yesterday and today and forever.
Hebrews 13:8 (ESV)

Read Together:

As we grow old together, we *change*; we become *different* compared to when we were young. The definition of **difference** is "a point or way in which people or things are not the same; an instance or point of unlikeness or dissimilarity." After almost 40 years of marriage, my wife and I have both undergone numerous changes, most notably physically, but also mentally and spiritually. There are *differences*, and not all of them are good or welcome. I am the first to admit that my body is much different today than it was when I was in my twenties (and not for the better!). There is little we can do to slow down the physical aging process. But what about our relationships? What differences are there in your relationship to your spouse? To your Lord? Have these relationships improved or have they gotten worse through the years? Today's introductory scripture passage reminds us that Jesus Christ does not change. He was perfect from the beginning, and he is no different today than he was yesterday or will be in the future. Likewise for us, while it is not possible to avoid *negative* differences in some of the *physical* aspects of our being, we should always strive for *positive* differences in the *spiritual* aspects of our being and in our relationship with our spouse and

46

with our Lord. Fortunately, it is possible to have spiritual growth and improvement even while our bodies degenerate with age.

As you and your spouse change as you grow old together, always strive for *positive* differences in the areas that are most important, namely, spiritual and relational.

Discuss Together:
1. Think about and list some of the differences in your relationship with your spouse that have occurred since you first married.
2. Discuss a specific aspect of your relationship with your spouse that has improved over the years. How has it improved? Did the improvement come naturally, or did you have to work at it?
3. Discuss a specific aspect of your relationship with God that has improved over the years. How has it improved? Did the improvement come naturally, or did you have to work at it?
4. Discuss ways in which both you and your spouse can improve in your relationship with each other and with the Lord.
5. The gospel is about grace and forgiveness. Forgive each other for those times when you may not have been as accepting or tolerant of the changes in your spouse over the years.

Study Together:
Study **Hebrews 1:8-12**, which describes how everything in the universe changes but God does not! Discuss the good and bad of change. With the Lord's help, your walk with the Lord will change for the better as you grow old together.

Pray Together:
Pray with your spouse and ask for the Lord's help in accepting each other's differences.

22. Materialism

Growing Old Together...

By John M. Cimbala, 2019

Frank: Can I buy a Corvette?
Ethel: The only reason a man buys a Corvette is to impress women.
Frank: (proudly) Well, *I* don't *need* a car or anything *else* to impress women!
Ethel: Good! Then that settles it... ☺.
Frank: ☹ ... Umm ...Ooops! ...☹

Artwork by Helen Dickey

Take care, and be on your guard against all covetousness, for one's life does not consist in the abundance of his possessions.
Luke 12:15 (ESV)

Read Together:
Do you covet material possessions? We all like to have nice things, but the Bible warns against materialism. The definition of ***materialism*** is "a tendency to consider material possessions as more important than spiritual values." Now that is an amazing definition, and I was surprised to see it in a secular dictionary! But how do you determine how much is *too* much? Even worse, how do you decide what car, house, etc., to buy if one spouse is more materialistic than the other? Both extremes are harmful. If you are too materialistic, it can come at the expense of your spiritual values, as the dictionary says. Conversely, if you care too little about your possessions, you may find it difficult to function in our society. You may even fall victim to *pride*, thinking you are more spiritual than someone else because you have a smaller house, an older car, an older cellphone... In marriage there is the additional complication that the husband's spending priorities (cars, sports, sports cars...) may not align with the wife's priorities (nice clothes, hair styling, new furniture...). One may fault the other for being materialistic when in reality you are *both* materialistic but for different material! Jesus reminds us in today's introductory scripture passage that a person's life does not consist in the

abundance of his or her possessions, but rather in the fullness of life in Christ.

Be sensitive to your spouse's spending priorities as you grow old together. Enjoy your possessions, but don't let them lead you into materialism.

Discuss Together:
1. What is your most important material possession? Do you regard it as "more important than spiritual values," as in the above definition of materialism? If so, what should you do about it?
2. How would you react if your most important possession were suddenly taken away without your approval?
3. Think of a material possession that you value greatly but that has little or no value to your spouse. Is this possession having an adverse effect on your marriage? If so, are you willing to give it up?
4. Think of a material possession that you *desire* but do not have, and that your spouse does not equally desire and has expressed a wish that it not be purchased. Why do you desire it so much? Is there resentment toward your spouse because he or she is not in agreement with you about owning that possession? If so, discuss together how to deal with this issue.
5. The gospel is about grace and forgiveness. Forgive each other for times when you valued material possessions more than your relationship with your spouse.

Study Together:
Study **Acts 4:32-37**, which discusses how Christians in the early church had everything in common. Discuss the advantages and disadvantages of such a system. Discuss how well (or not so well) you would do in a system like that. With the Lord's help, you, like the Apostle Paul, can be content in any situation, whether you have many or few possessions.

Pray Together:
Pray with your spouse and ask for the Lord's help in not being materialistic.

23. Consideration

Growing Old Together...   By John M. Cimbala, 2019

Frank: (After Ethel pours the last bit of milk into a glass) Why don't you just drink from the jug?

Ethel: Because I don't eat like an animal.

Frank: But *I* sometimes drink the last drops of milk directly from the jug.

Ethel: Like I said...

Frank: ...☺ ...☹

Artwork by Helen Dickey

Husbands, in the same way be considerate as you live with your wives, and treat them with respect as the weaker partner and as heirs with you of the gracious gift of life, so that nothing will hinder your prayers.
1 Peter 3:7 (NIV)

Read Together:

Have you become *less* considerate of your spouse as you grow old together? If so, perhaps it's time for a refresher course. The definition of **consideration** is "sympathetic regard or respect; thoughtfulness for others." In today's introductory scripture passage, Peter tells husbands to be considerate of their wives and to treat them with respect. This was rather radical in Peter's time since women were generally *not* treated with respect or honor. He reminds men that their wives are co-heirs with them of the gracious gift of life. Peter even warns husbands that, if they are *not* considerate toward their wives, it can hinder their prayers! And, as co-heirs of the Kingdom of God, the same principle applies to wives. We both need to treat our spouse with consideration. What are some practical ways we can be considerate of our spouse? Husbands: Take your dirty dishes to the sink. If your wife is finished eating, remove *her* used plates also. Put the toilet seat down when finished in the bathroom. Offer to do some additional chores around the house, particularly those that you know she finds unpleasant or difficult. Wives: Ask for his opinion on matters of concern to you. Help him with his chores. Speak well of him in public. Encourage his manliness; for example, my wife is not ashamed to admit that she is physically weaker than I, and I enjoy opening jars for her, reaching high into the cupboard to get something, and doing other small acts that show kindness and consideration. But sometimes she asks me to help at inconvenient times; I admit that I do not always help *cheerfully*. At such times I need to remind myself of Peter's words.

Be considerate of your spouse as you grow old together. You will never regret having shown consideration, and, according to Peter, this will also enhance your prayer life.

Discuss Together:
1. Today's introductory scripture passage warns us that our prayers could be hindered if we are not considerate! In what ways does this warning motivate you to be more considerate toward your spouse?
2. Think of something your spouse does that you feel is inconsiderate. Why did you choose that particular item?
3. In light of the items that you and your spouse chose for the previous question, without being confrontational, work together on ways you can be more considerate of each other in these matters.
4. Does being considerate toward others, and especially toward your spouse, come naturally to you? If not, think of ways you can improve in this area.
5. The gospel is about grace and forgiveness. Forgive each other for times you have not been considerate toward each other, just as in Christ, God forgave you.

Study Together:
Study **Ruth 3**, which describes the kindness and consideration of Boaz toward Ruth and her mother-in-law Naomi. Discuss the impact of these acts of kindness. With the Lord's help, you will always show kindness and consideration for your spouse as you grow old together.

Pray Together:
Pray with your spouse and ask for the Lord's help in showing more consideration for each other.

24. Jealousy

Laugh Together:

Growing Old Together...   By John M. Cimbala, 2019

Frank: (proudly) I was eating at that new restaurant today, and a pretty girl smiled at me.
Ethel: Uh huh. That's nice.
Frank: Are you jealous?
Ethel: Yes.
Frank: ☺
Ethel: I'm jealous that *I* didn't get to eat lunch there.
Frank: ...☹

Artwork by Helen Dickey

... love is strong as death, jealousy is fierce as the grave. Its flashes are flashes of fire, the very flame of the Lord.
Song of Solomon 8:6 (ESV)

Read Together:

Are you ever jealous of someone better looking than you? Or, as you grow old together and your bodies begin to lose those last remnants of youthfulness, are you ever jealous of the *spouse* of someone younger and better looking than *your* spouse? The definition of **jealousy** is "the state or feeling of being jealous or envious; covetousness; resentment." Jealousy is especially damaging to your spouse when it becomes obvious. Like any other normal man, I appreciate physical beauty in a woman. My wife admires female loveliness as well, and we usually agree when a woman is particularly beautiful. But she has a way of knowing when I appreciate another woman's beauty a little *too* much. She'll say something such as "stop staring" or "don't overdo it." Today's introductory scripture passage was penned by Solomon; he contrasts love with jealousy. He reminds us that, although love is as strong as death, jealousy is as fierce as the grave. He says that jealousy's flashes are flashes of fire. Solomon's comments about jealousy remind me of the words of the Apostle James about the tongue; he says in James 3:5, "*How great a forest is set ablaze by such a small fire!*" A little jealousy can do a lot of damage. So how can you avoid being jealous? A state of conscious gratefulness for the spouse who has faithfully stood by your side all these years, through trials and hard times as well as through fun times can help overcome jealous feelings. An attitude of gratitude overcomes jealousy.

Be grateful for the spouse the Lord has given you, and do not let a spark of jealousy fan into a destructive flame as you grow old together.

Discuss Together:
1. Reflect deeply upon this: Does anything good ever come from jealousy? Discuss.
2. Name someone of whom you used to be jealous, at an earlier stage of your life, maybe even before your marriage. Why were you jealous of that person? Discuss how you got over it.
3. Name someone of whom you are jealous *now* (or recently), and discuss *why*.
4. Together, work on some specific ways you can decrease (or, better yet, *remove*) the specific jealousy of the previous question.
5. The gospel is about grace and forgiveness. Forgive each other for times when you have been jealous of others, especially if it hurt your spouse's feelings.

Study Together:
Study **Genesis 37**, which describes the intense jealousy of Joseph's brothers. Discuss how jealousy impacted so many lives, but how Joseph was able to forgive. With the Lord's help, such a deep jealousy will never take root in you.

Pray Together:
Pray with your spouse and ask for the Lord's help in maintaining an attitude of gratitude so that jealousy does not hold a grip on you.

25. Sincerity

Growing Old Together...

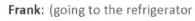

By John M. Cimbala, 2019

Frank: (going to the refrigerator to get drinks) Do you want milk or water?

Ethel: Milk, please.

Frank: Sorry... we are out of milk.

Ethel: Then why did you *ask* me?

Frank: I was hoping you would choose water, and then you'd think I was being nice. ☺

Ethel: ...☹

Artwork by Helen Dickey

For our boast is this, ... that we behaved in the world with simplicity and godly sincerity, not by earthly wisdom but by the grace of God.
2 Corinthians 1:12 (ESV)

Read Together:

Do you always act with sincerity toward your spouse? The definition of **sincerity** is "the quality of being free from pretense, deceit, or hypocrisy; genuineness; integrity." I made a commitment even before I got married that I would never lie to my wife. And I can honestly say that I never have, nor has she ever lied to me; our marriage is based on honesty as it must be. Is it possible to be *honest* but not *sincere*? I believe so. Honesty involves telling the truth; sincerity goes beyond honesty – sincerity involves telling the *whole* truth and leaving nothing out. I admit that sometimes I withhold information from my wife. Sometimes I say something honestly but leave out some of the details that might make her upset or get me busted or "incriminate" me. In today's introductory scripture passage Paul states that he and his fellow evangelists behaved with godly sincerity. From where did this sincerity come? As Paul says, not by earthly wisdom but by the grace of God. Earthly wisdom tells us that our happiness is of primary concern; if we are a little insincere sometimes, it doesn't hurt anyone, especially if we are honest. But godly

54

wisdom teaches us that sincerity means being sincere all the time, even in little things. Such sincerity comes only by God's grace.

By the grace of God, always behave with godly sincerity toward your spouse as you grow old together.

Discuss Together:
1. How would you define honesty? How would you define sincerity? Discuss the differences between these two qualities.
2. Time to confess: Think of a time when you were *honest* but not *sincere* with your spouse. Discuss why you acted that way, and ask for forgiveness.
3. Think again about the previous question. Discuss together some specific ways you can avoid insincerity in similar situations in the future.
4. In the "read together" part of this devotional, a distinction was made between worldly wisdom and godly wisdom and between worldly sincerity and godly sincerity. What actions can you take to ensure that you have the latter rather than the former?
5. The gospel is about grace and forgiveness. Forgive each other for the times you have not been sincere with your spouse.

Study Together:
Study **2 Timothy 1:2-14**, in which the Apostle Paul encourages his timid young disciple, Timothy, to be strong and to maintain his faith. Paul mentions Timothy's mother and grandmother, who modeled sincere faith to young Timothy. Discuss your role as parent, grandparent, or elder in training the next generation to have sincerity. With the Lord's help, he will use you to encourage younger people in their sincere faith.

Pray Together:
Pray with your spouse and ask for the Lord's help in maintaining complete and total honesty *and* sincerity in your marriage.

26. Maturity

But solid food is for the mature, for those who have their powers of discernment trained by constant practice to distinguish good from evil.
Hebrews 5:14 (ESV)

Read Together:

Do you show maturity in *all* aspects of your life? The definition of **maturity** is "the quality of behaving mentally and emotionally like an adult; fully developed." It is easy to see signs of maturity in our *physical* bodies as we age: Our hair turns gray or disappears (in my case a little of *both*). We get wrinkly skin and age spots. Our hearing and eyesight fade. Our strength declines. But what about maturity in our *spiritual* life? Spiritual maturity is harder to define, yet we know instinctively when someone is *not* spiritually mature. The author of Hebrews was lamenting about the spiritual immaturity of those to whom he wrote. In the sentence just prior to today's introductory scripture passage he writes, *"You need milk, not solid food, for everyone who lives on milk is unskilled in the word of righteousness."* These people were adults physically, but in spiritual matters they were infants. They were still drinking milk (the basic principles of the faith) even though by this time they should have been eating meat (deeper, more extensive principles of the faith). According to the author of Hebrews, this kind of maturity comes only from constant practice. In marriage we naturally mature and age physically. It is a wonderful blessing, though, when both husband and wife also mature *spiritually*, not only "dining" on the meat, but also *feeding* each other meat, not simply milk.

Embrace each other's maturity, both physical and spiritual, as you grow old together.

Discuss Together:
1. Name some specific ways in which you have matured *physically* since your wedding. Have any of these been positive or beneficial? If so, in what way?
2. Which aspects of physical maturing are most annoying, debilitating, or frightening to you? Why?
3. How would you define spiritual maturity? Discuss and compare your definition with that of your spouse. Work together until you agree on a definition that satisfies both of you.
4. Compare your level of spiritual maturity on your wedding day with your level today. Name some specific ways in which you have matured *spiritually* during the years of your marriage. If you fall short in this area, discuss some constructive ways you can aim for greater spiritual maturity.
5. The gospel is about grace and forgiveness. Forgive each other for the times you have not shown spiritual maturity.

Study Together:
Study **Hebrews 6:1-12**, which describes spiritual maturity in God's people and which compares and contrasts the consequences for those who are and are not spiritually mature. Discuss some of the warnings in this passage. With the Lord's help, you can continue to grow in spiritual maturity even as your physical bodies grow old.

Pray Together:
Pray with your spouse and ask for the Lord's help in becoming more spiritually mature so that you can enjoy the "meat" of the Christian life, not just the "milk."

27. Support

Laugh Together:

Growing Old Together...   By John M. Cimbala, 2019

Frank: Remember that song,
"You are the wind
beneath my wings."
Ethel: Yes.
Frank: Am I still the wind
beneath *your* wings?
Ethel: Not really. Now you are
more like hot air.
Frank: ...☺...

Artwork by Helen Dickey

They confronted me in the day of my calamity, but the LORD was my support.
Psalm 18:18 (ESV)

Read Together:

When you face problems or trouble, from whom do you get *support*? The definition of **support** is "a thing that bears the weight of something or keeps it upright." Husbands and wives must support each other, and this includes all kinds of support – financial, emotional, spiritual. I am reminded of our wedding vows, "...in sickness and in health..." We should be thankful for the support of a loving spouse, and we should do everything in our power to support our spouse in turn. As the above definition states, we need to bear the weight of each other's problems and keep each other upright. However, we also need to remember that our spouse's support may not always be there for us; death or illness or dementia may eventually remove that support. So we need to be careful not to rely on our spouse for *all* of our support. Today's introductory scripture passage reminds us that the *Lord* needs to be our ultimate support. The Lord, whose support never waivers because of his omnipotence, is the only one who can bear the weight of all of our burdens. The Lord is not subject to the physical and mental limitations of humankind. Jesus said in Matthew 11:28-30, *"Come to me, all who labor and are heavy laden, and I will give you rest. Take my yoke upon you, and* *learn from me, for I am gentle and lowly in heart, and you will find rest for your souls. For my yoke is easy, and my burden is light."* I am comforted to know that we can always rely on the Lord to be the wind beneath our wings.

Support each other as you grow old together. Always trust in the Lord Jesus Christ, though, to be your ultimate and unfailing support.

Discuss Together:
1. Reflect on an incident or matter in which your spouse provided much needed support during a time when you really needed it. Thank him or her for that support!
2. Is there something happening *now* for which you could really use some extra support from your spouse? Talk it over with each other, and list some specific actions that you both can take to support each other in this matter.
3. Think about and discuss what Jesus meant when he said that you will find rest for your souls. What does it mean for your soul to be at rest?
4. Together, think about the supports on which you rely. Do you maintain a healthy balance between support from your spouse, support from others, and support from the Lord? If the balance is not healthy, talk about ways to improve.
5. The gospel is about grace and forgiveness. Forgive each other for those times when you really could have used more support from your spouse.

Study Together:
Study **Romans 11:11-24**, in which the Apostle Paul makes an analogy between people coming into the Kingdom and the grafting of olive branches. Discuss what this analogy means to you. With the Lord's help, you will learn to rely more on the support of the Lord, as Paul reminds us in Verse 18, "....remember it is not you who support the root, but the root that supports you."

Pray Together:
Pray with your spouse and ask for the Lord's help in supporting each other. Also pray for discernment about how to balance your support.

28. Laziness

Laugh Together:

Growing Old Together...

By John M. Cimbala, 2019

Frank: (sitting at the table) I need a spoon to eat this.

Ethel: ...☺ ...Well, you *are* fully capable of walking over and getting one *yourself*, you know.

Frank: (walks into kitchen) Ummm...Which drawer are the spoons in?

Ethel: ☹

Artwork by Helen Dickey

How long will you lie there, O sluggard? When will you arise from your sleep? A little sleep, a little slumber, a little folding of the hands to rest, and poverty will come upon you like a robber, and want like an armed man.

Proverbs 6:9-11 (ESV)

Read Together:

Do you have a problem with laziness? The definition of *laziness* is "disinclined to work, activity, or exertion; slothfulness; desiring idleness." I am by nature *not* a lazy person. But I admit that I am more inclined toward laziness when I am with my wife than when I am at work or with others. I can think of many reasons (which sometimes means *excuses*) for this. When I am alone with my wife, I am usually tired from the day's work, so I feel "entitled" to rest. Rest is essential and well deserved, especially after a hard day's work. We must be careful, however, not to let rest turn into laziness. In our marriage, we have traditional gender roles. For example, I fix things in the house and carry heavy items for her; she cooks and does the dishes. I maintain the cars, the lawn, and the outside of the house; she does our finances, does most of the shopping, and cleans the inside of the house. So, when I want or need something that involves "her job," I am more inclined to be lazy and let *her* do it rather than take the initiative to do it myself. This is neither loving nor considerate, and I need to work harder at correcting this character flaw.

God does not want us to be lazy, and the Bible contains many warnings against laziness. Today's introductory scripture passage, for example, (which applies to paid employment, not marriage) warns that poverty comes to the lazy sluggard. Laziness in marriage may lead to a different kind of poverty.

Don't "justify" your laziness. Instead, always look for ways to please your spouse and to make your spouse's life more pleasant. Don't fall into the trap of laziness as you grow old together.

Discuss Together:
1. Re-read today's introductory scripture passage verse from Proverbs 6. Discuss how to properly balance work and rest. At what point does resting cross over from necessity to laziness?
2. Reflect on a time when you did *not* do something for your spouse because of laziness. Confess this to your spouse. How did you justify your inaction at the time?
3. Apologize for your inaction of the previous question.
4. Brainstorming together, think of a phrase that both of you can remember and put into practice whenever you *kindly* ask for help. For example, *Good*: "Honey, I could really use your help here, please." *Not so good*: "Stop being a lazy bum and help me here!"
5. The gospel is about grace and forgiveness. Forgive each other for the times you acted (or *didn't* act) due to laziness.

Study Together:
Study **2 Thessalonians 3:6-15**, which discusses how Christians are to treat fellow believers who are idle or lazy. Discuss how to draw the line between *discipline* for laziness (V. 10, "... *If anyone is not willing to work, let him not eat.*") and *encouragement* (V. 12, "...*encourage in the Lord Jesus Christ to do their work quietly and to earn their own living.*"). With the Lord's help, you will overcome any tendencies toward laziness with which you struggle, especially those that affect your spouse.

Pray Together:
Pray with your spouse, asking for the Lord's help in overcoming the tendency to be lazy, especially in those things that have the most impact on your spouse.

29. Pride

Growing Old Together...   By John M. Cimbala, 2019

Frank: (After a brief argument)
Well...I think that some
women would *kill* to have
a husband like me.
Ethel: You're probably right.
Frank: ☺
Ethel: But some *other* women
would *kill* a husband like
you.
Frank: ...☺ ...☹

Artwork by Helen Dickey

One's pride will bring him low, but he who is lowly in spirit will obtain honor.
Proverbs 29:23 (ESV)

Read Together:

Are you *proud*? The definition of **pride** is "a high or inordinate opinion of one's own dignity, importance, merit, or superiority." Pride (haughty eyes) is one of the seven things that God hates, as listed by Solomon in Chapter 6 of Proverbs. In fact, it is the first one on the list! The Bible is filled with warnings about pride and how pride leads to destruction. What about pride in your *marriage*? Do you get angry when your spouse tries to correct you, especially when he or she is *right*? I do. That is pride poking up its ugly head. I often get on my wife's nerves because of my perfectionism, along with many of my other flaws. When she brings up an aspect of my behavior about which she desires to communicate, or starts to correct me for something I did or said, my immediate *natural* tendency is to become defensive and make clear to her that I can do *what* I want *when* I want, and that I don't need *her* approval. As the above definition of pride shows, this is the result of my inordinate opinion of myself. Proverbs 16:18 says, *"Pride goes before destruction, and a haughty spirit before a fall."* I am too proud to admit how many times I have experienced this, especially in my marriage. When my wife corrects me and I lash back at her, it usually does not end well. I feel bad and guilty, and I eventually realize that she is right... most of the time.

Everything we have is a gift from God, so we shouldn't have a prideful attitude about *anything*. Respect your spouse, accept correction and advice, and quash your prideful attitude as you grow old together.

Discuss Together:
1. Reflect on a talent, accomplishment, or activity that tends to induce a prideful attitude. Ask your spouse whether he or she has noticed this as well. Discuss how to quash this tendency.
2. Ask your spouse to identify *another* issue for which he or she has noticed a prideful attitude (something other than the one identified in the previous question). Perhaps it is something you had not noticed in yourself. Discuss ways to avoid becoming prideful when in similar situations in the future.
3. Discuss the fine line between accepting healthy praise from others and becoming arrogant or filled with pride. How can you avoid crossing this line?
4. Discuss how you can improve the way you correct your spouse when you feel it is necessary. In particular, how can you *gently* help your spouse quash his or her prideful attitude without stirring up anger?
5. The gospel is about grace and forgiveness. Forgive each other for the times you have expressed a prideful attitude.

Study Together:
Study **Daniel 4:4-37**, which discusses the pride, downfall, and restoration of King Nebuchadnezzar. This is an extreme example of the consequences of pride. Why do you think God made Nebuchadnezzar go through such a severe trial? With the Lord's help, you will never become so prideful that the Lord needs to be harsh in correcting you.

Pray Together:
Pray with your spouse and ask for the Lord's help in controlling your prideful attitude. Pray also for discernment in recognizing pride in yourself and in your spouse.

30. Banality

Growing Old Together...   By John M. Cimbala, 2019

Ethel: (irritated because Frank is goofing off) Could you please act your age?

Frank: I don't know how.

Ethel: What do you mean you don't know how?

Frank: I was never this age before! ...☺

Ethel: ☹

Artwork by Helen Dickey

Then I considered all that my hands had done and the toil I had expended in doing it, and behold, all was vanity and a striving after wind, and there was nothing to be gained under the sun.
Ecclesiastes 2:11 (ESV)

Read Together:

Do the daily tasks of life sometimes seem repetitious, boring, not worthwhile, or even *banal*? The definition of **banality** is "triteness, staleness, unimaginativeness, lack of originality; devoid of freshness." The Bible does not use the words banal or banality. The closest word I found is "vanity," which Solomon uses often in his writings. In today's introductory scripture passage, he laments that all his work and toil is vanity, a striving after the wind, and without benefit. This is banality. The first thing that comes to *my* mind when I think of the word banal is certain TV shows. I don't regularly watch much TV, but when I happen upon some shows, I notice that they are often centered on trivial or foolish matters, often sexual in nature. The annoying laugh tracks make things worse; we don't even get to decide for ourselves whether something is funny or not. In such situations, I find myself saying out loud, "Banal!" and then walking away.

As you may have guessed by now, I like humor. My problem is that I often "humorize" *everything*, which may annoy others. I need to learn to strike a balance between being serious and being humorous. We all need to refrain from trivializing and banalizing life. Much of what we do daily, weekly, monthly... is repetitious and stale, even banal. Be careful not to let banality affect your attitude toward your spouse as you grow old together.

Discuss Together:

1. How do *you* define banality? Where do you draw the line beyond which something that at first seems to be humorous, fun, and wholesome becomes banal?
2. Reflect on an incident or activity which, looking back, crossed the line and became banal. Why did you continue in the activity, and what should you have done differently?
3. Discuss some indicators of banality. In other words, how can you recognize when a conversation or activity is starting to degenerate into banality?
4. Discuss some practical ways for you and your spouse to avoid being drawn into banal activities in the future. It may be useful to think of a code word to use when you are in public to discretely tell your spouse that the activity is getting banal and that the two of you should leave.
5. The gospel is about grace and forgiveness. Forgive each other for wasted time – time that could have been spent encouraging each other.

Study Together:

Study **Ephesians 5:1-20**, which discusses how we are to live our lives as Christians, along with a list of things we are supposed to avoid. Among this list is "foolish talk." Discuss how to define foolish talk. Is this the same as the banality of today's devotional? With the Lord's help, you will be imitators of God and walk in love (as Paul tells us in **Ephesians 5:1-2**).

Pray Together:

Pray with your spouse and ask for the Lord's help as we strive for a good balance between humor and seriousness and as we try to avoid banality.

31. Submission

Growing Old Together...   By John M. Cimbala, 2019

Ethel: I'm thankful that you don't demand to always have the last word.
Frank: ☺
Ethel: In fact, I'm *most* thankful when you have the last *two* words!
Frank: ☺...Which two words?
Ethel: "Yes, dear." ...☺
Frank: 😐 ...☹

Artwork by Helen Dickey

... submitting to one another out of reverence for Christ. Wives, submit to your own husbands, as to the Lord. For the husband is the head of the wife even as Christ is the head of the church.
Ephesians 5:21-23 (ESV)

Read Together:

Are you submissive to your spouse? The definition of **submission** is "accepting or yielding to the will or authority of another person." In today's introductory scripture passage, wives are commanded to submit to their husbands. Some women may take offense at this. They are quick to point out that the Bible says elsewhere that men and women are equal in God's eyes. For example, Galatians 3:28, *"There is neither ... male nor female, for you are all one in Christ Jesus."* How do we reconcile these apparently contradictory statements? We need to understand submission in terms of *authority* rather than *importance* or *ability*. Men and women are spiritually equal, but God assigned authority to the *husband*. Here is an army analogy: a sergeant has authority over a corporal, not because he is better, smarter, or stronger, but because he has been *appointed* to the higher rank. So it is with husbands and wives. When God administered punishment to Adam and Eve after their sin, he established an authority structure with man as the head. He said to the woman, *"Your desire shall be toward your husband, but he shall rule over you."* So, even though men and women are spiritually equal in God's eyes, the man has been given authority in marriage. Men, we need to take this role seriously, being willing to even lay down our lives for our wives, as Christ did for the church.

As you grow old together, wives submit to your husbands, and husbands, love your wives.

Discuss Together:

1. Have you, husband, ever used the instructions from today's introductory scripture passage to force your wife to do something? If you cannot remember, perhaps your wife will. Discuss the results of that incident and how each of you felt at the time. How do you feel *now* about it?
2. Today's introductory scripture passage instructs wives to be submissive to their husbands, but does not give any details. Discuss specific areas in which wives should be submissive to their husband's leadership (assuming that the husband is a Christ-like leader).
3. In the first verse of today's introductory scripture passage, Paul instructs us to *submit to each other*. Discuss specific areas in which husbands and wives should have equal say, in other words where *"wives, submit to your husbands"* does *not* apply.
4. Read the rest of Chapter 5 of Ephesians, which deals with the *husband's* role. Which is harder, submission or love? Discuss why husbands may have the more difficult assignment here.
5. The gospel is about grace and forgiveness. Wife, forgive your husband for those times when he misused his authority. Husband, forgive your wife for those times when she refused biblically proper submission.

Study Together:

Study **Mark 10:35-45**, which discusses Jesus' reaction to James and John when they asked for special places of honor in heaven. Discuss what Jesus said to his disciples about *authority* in the last few verses of that passage. With the Lord's help, you will be empowered by the Holy Spirit to have a servant's attitude, imitating Jesus Christ.

Pray Together:

Pray with your spouse and ask for the Lord's help in understanding submission in a biblically correct way and then carrying it out.

32. Obsolescence

Laugh Together:

Growing Old Together...

By John M. Cimbala, 2019

Frank: (just home from work) What did *you* do today?

Ethel: I threw out some old, useless stuff that was sitting around the house.

Frank: ☺...Did you get *all* of it?

Ethel: ☺

Frank: Why are you looking at *me* like that? ...☺ ...☹

Ethel: ☺

Artwork by Helen Dickey

In speaking of a new covenant, he makes the first one obsolete. And what is becoming obsolete and growing old is ready to vanish away.
Hebrews 8:13 (ESV)

Read Together:

Do you ever feel obsolete? The definition of **obsolescence** is "the state, process, or condition of no longer being useful." Some things get obsolete very quickly, like cellphones and computer equipment. Other things, like automobiles and kitchen appliances, take many years or even decades to become obsolete. Eventually, nearly everything becomes old and useless and in need of replacement. When we clean out a closet or drawer, my wife and I find several obsolete items that we either throw away, give away, or stash away again, thinking that they may be useful... someday. What about *people*? As we age, tasks such as using a new computer, operating a new cellphone, setting up a new television system, etc., become harder to learn, and it is easy to feel obsolete. Today's introductory scripture passage reminds us that even *covenants* can become obsolete. When Christ came as the one sacrifice for all sins, a new covenant was established, making the first one obsolete. What about the *marriage* covenant? While acknowledging that there are legitimate reasons for divorce, many couples undergoing marital stress conclude that their marriage covenant is obsolete, so they break it and go their separate ways. But we are commanded to stay married until one of

68

us dies; the marriage covenant must not be broken or violated. Unless there is unrepentant adultery or abuse, the marriage covenant should *never* become obsolete as long as we are both alive.

Even though you may sometimes *feel* obsolete as you grow old together, you are not. In God's eyes, you are just getting closer to enjoying eternal fellowship with him!

Discuss Together:
1. Think back to a time when you felt obsolete. Discuss what role, if any, your spouse played during or leading up to that incident. Was he or she helpful afterward? Why or why not? How did that make you feel?
2. Discuss some specific things you and your spouse can do differently when times similar to those of the previous question arise in the future.
3. Discuss what frightens you most about getting old and no longer able to do the activities that make you feel useful. How can you help each other to not feel obsolete?
4. Take some time to renew your marriage vows to each other. Promise each other that your marriage covenant will *never* become obsolete as long as you both may live.
5. The gospel is about grace and forgiveness. Forgive each other for the times your spouse made you feel useless or obsolete.

Study Together:
Study **Job 31:1-12**, which is a small portion of Job's defense against the accusations against him by his "friends." Discuss the importance Job places on his covenant to his wife, especially in verses 1 and 9-12. Pray that you, like Job, will never think of your spouse as obsolete. With the Lord's help, you will never entertain the thought of tossing your marriage covenant aside to seek the affection of someone younger.

Pray Together:
Pray with your spouse and ask for the Lord's help in keeping your marriage covenant, especially when you feel obsolete.

33. Health

Laugh Together:

Growing Old Together...   By John M. Cimbala, 2019

Ethel: (looking at Frank's arms) Why are you so hairy?

Frank: Probably because I have such good circulation. ☺

Ethel: Then why don't you have hair on top of your *head*?

Frank: I guess I don't get much blood flowing up there.

Ethel: I could have told you *that*! ☺

Frank: ☺ ...☹

Artwork by Helen Dickey

Beloved, I pray that all may go well with you and that you may be in good health, as it goes well with your soul.
3 John 1:2 (ESV)

Read Together:

Do you worry about health? The definition of **health** is "soundness of body or mind; freedom from disease or ailment." As we age, our bodies weaken and we (slowly) lose health. I exercise regularly, eat nutritiously, and take care of my body. But when I compare the state of my body to the above definition of health (especially the part about freedom from ailment), perhaps I am not all that healthy. Every time I do yard work or bend or twist my body in some unusual way, I feel ailments in my joints and muscles! This is all part of growing old, I suppose. It is interesting that the dictionary also defines health of the *mind* (soundness of mind). As I have alluded to several times in this devotional series, our minds lose health too, and we become forgetful as we age. Today's introductory scripture passage is from a personal letter from the old Apostle John to his dear friend Gaius. John prays that his friend may be in good health *and* that it may go well with his *soul*. This reminds me that even though our bodies and minds are destined to fail us, our *souls* can remain strong even to the hour of our death. Our soul is the part of us that is immortal, the essence of who we *are*. The soul goes immediately into the presence of the Lord Jesus Christ at death. As Christians, we also know that our souls will one day be joined to a new resurrected body. Then we will be in perfect health! Forever!

Try your best to remain healthy in body and mind as you grow old together. But keep in mind that it is your *soul* that will live forever.

Discuss Together:
1. Discuss some of your fears about losing physical and/or mental health as you age.
2. How do you cope with the aging process? Discuss ways in which you can help each other in this area as you grow old together. Specifically, discuss the fears you identified in the first question.
3. It is inevitable that we lose health in our bodies (and often also in our minds) as we age. What about your *soul*? Is your soul healthy? How do *you* define a healthy soul, and how can you keep your soul's health from declining?
4. We exercise our bodies to stay healthy. Are there exercises for your *mind* to keep it healthy? What about your *soul*?
5. The gospel is about grace and forgiveness. Forgive each other for the times when you did not make the health of your spouse a high priority.

Study Together:
Study **Deuteronomy 4:1-40**, which is part of Moses' speech to the stubborn Israelites as they wandered in the wilderness. Though we were not there as Moses spoke, his encouragements still apply to us today. Discuss which of Moses' encouragements from thousands of years ago are most impacting in your life and your marriage. Read verse 9 aloud and discuss this verse together; list some specific things you can do to obey this particular command. With the Lord's help, you and your spouse can encourage each other to, as Moses says, *"keep your soul diligently."*

Pray Together:
Pray with your spouse and ask for the Lord's help in maintaining healthy bodies, minds, and most importantly, souls.

34. Improvement

Growing Old Together...   By John M. Cimbala, 2019

Frank: Do you remember our marriage vows?

Ethel: I remember the part about "for better or for worse."

Frank: Well that part came true. Over the years, you got better! ☺

Ethel: Thanks! ☺ ...And you got worse...

Frank: ...☺ Don't say it! ...☹

Ethel: ☺

Artwork by Helen Dickey

...Vashti is never again to come before King Ahasuerus. And let the king give her royal position to another who is better than she.
Esther 1:19 (ESV)

Read Together:

Is there any area in your marriage in which you are *improving*? The definition of ***improvement*** is "becoming better; the process of bringing into a more valuable or desirable condition; an advance in excellence or achievement." When we marry, we state our vows "for better or for worse." As we age, some things naturally get worse, like our physical bodies. Some things, on the other hand, should get *better*. How we love each other, how we sacrifice for each other, how we build each other up, and how we spur each other on to spiritual maturity are examples of components of marriage that can grow and develop with time. These (and other) aspects of our marriage should be *improving* as the years go by. Today's introductory scripture passage describes how Queen Vashti was dethroned because of her disobedience to King Ahasuerus. His counselors urged him to look for someone better who would replace her. We don't know the details about their marriage, but I'm sure this estrangement did not happen overnight. I suspect that neither Ahasuerus nor Vashti worked on improving their marriage. Sadly, this is true for many couples today, including Christian couples. Improvement takes work. If we make little or no effort at improving our marriage, it will inevitably get worse; it will naturally decline rather than improve.

As you grow old together, there are some aspects of your life that naturally deteriorate and others that should improve. Strive to always get better, not worse, in these areas as you grow old together.

Discuss Together:
1. Encourage each other by listing a few aspects of your spouse about which you have noticed improvement through the years since you first married.
2. Name one specific area, behavior, attitude, etc. in which you would like to see improvement in *yourself*. Then together come up with ways to work toward this goal.
3. Name one specific area, behavior, attitude, etc. in which you would like to see improvement in your *spouse* (something not already mentioned by your spouse in the previous question). Then together come up with ways to work toward this goal.
4. Reflect together on the part of your wedding vows, "for better or for worse." Praise the Lord that you have stayed together all these years, even through the "worse."
5. The gospel is about grace and forgiveness. Forgive each other for the times when you criticized your spouse for his or her failure to improve in certain areas.

Study Together:
Study **Ephesians 5:21-33**, which discusses how wives and husbands are to treat each other. Identify one specific area from this passage in which you should improve in your relationship with your spouse. Discuss specific action items to help both you and your spouse as you strive to improve in this area. With the Lord's help, you will be given strength, endurance, and patience to follow through and implement these improvements.

Pray Together:
Pray with your spouse and ask for the Lord's help in improving your attitudes, the way you treat each other, how you encourage each other, etc.

35. Reminiscence

<u>**Laugh Together**</u>:

Growing Old Together...

By John M. Cimbala, 2019

Frank: (looking at old photos)
Wow! We were really *hot*
when we were young.
Ethel: I suppose so.
Frank: Do you think I'll ever be
hot again?
Ethel: I can make you *really* hot
again!
Frank: ☺...♥ Sounds exciting!
♥...How?
Ethel: When you die, I'll
cremate you. ☺
Frank: ...☺ ...☹

Artwork by Helen Dickey

Remember also your Creator in the days of your youth, before ... the years draw near of which you will say, "I have no pleasure in them."
Ecclesiastes 12:1 (ESV)

<u>**Read Together**</u>:

Do you like to reminisce? The definition of ***reminiscence*** is "the act or process of recalling or remembering past experiences; the enjoyable recollection of past events." Old photos tend to cause *me* to reminisce. When I look back at fun activities my family and I experienced during our younger years, I have happy recollections. Upon reflection, though, pictures are taken of happy times, not sad ones, so it is natural to re-enjoy those old pictures... to reminisce. Of course, we were better-looking and healthier 20 or 30 years ago, and remembering those days can also make us yearn to be young again. Too much of this kind of yearning is not healthy, especially in marriage; it can lead to unhappiness, or even depression, about our present state or that of our spouse. We must be careful not to reminisce about the past so much that we no longer enjoy and appreciate the present. In today's introductory scripture passage, Solomon gives wise advice along these lines. He admonishes us to remember our Creator in the days of our youth, *before* we get too old to enjoy what we have now. So, the next time you look at old pictures, go ahead and reminisce; praise God that you have good memories of days gone by. Just don't *dwell* on them.

You will never be young again, but as you grow old together, thank the Lord that you can recall happy times when you *were* young.

Discuss Together:
1. Think back to a time or event in your marriage that was most enjoyable and about which you sometimes reminisce. Discuss what in particular made that time or event so memorable.
2. It is likely that the items mentioned by you and your spouse in the previous question are not repeatable. Discuss, however, something that the two of you can do together *now* to help you reminisce with more enjoyment.
3. Plan some activities for the near future (maybe even today!) through which the two of you can make *new* memories. Enjoy those thoughts now and reminisce upon them in the future.
4. Get out an old photo album, and look through the pictures together. Discuss some of the warm memories brought back by these pictures.
5. The gospel is about grace and forgiveness. Forgive each other for the times when you have not made an effort to reminisce about the enjoyable events you and your spouse have shared together.

Study Together:
Study **Exodus 13:1-16**, in which God tells the Israelites to remember the day they were freed from slavery in Egypt. Discuss whether or not they followed God's command. Hint: They complained often and reminisced about how good they had it back in Egypt! With the Lord's help, you and your spouse will not dwell on the past, but rather reminisce on the joyful moments the Lord has given you in your marriage.

Pray Together:
Pray with your spouse and ask for the Lord's help to create new memories together about which both of you can reminisce in the future.

36. Toil

Growing Old Together...   By John M. Cimbala, 2019

Ethel: (looking out the window at the snow) You need to shovel the driveway.

Frank: But I'm watching the Steeler game!

Ethel: Well, the snow won't shovel itself! ...☺

Frank: Well, the TV won't watch itself either! ☺

Ethel: You think you're so funny. ☺

Artwork by Helen Dickey

Sweet is the sleep of a laborer, whether he eats little or much, but the full stomach of the rich will not let him sleep.
Ecclesiastes 5:12 (ESV)

Read Together:

Do you work, or do you *toil*? The definition of ***toil*** is "hard and continuous work; exhausting labor or effort; a laborious or fatiguing task." Work becomes toil when it is exhausting or laborious. We naturally attempt to keep our work from becoming toil. Though we may complain about work, it is well known that work is actually *good* for us. In today's introductory scripture passage, Solomon says that a laborer sleeps well while a rich person who does not have to work gets insomnia. Even Adam and Eve had to work before the Fall. But their work was not *toil* (fatiguing labor). Only after Adam's sin did God bring forth thorns and thistles that caused his work to become toilsome, sweaty labor. Chores like shoveling snow and mowing the grass can also be toilsome at times, especially as we age and physical work becomes more challenging. *Your* work may not involve thorns or sweat. You may sit at a desk, typing on a keyboard all day. While not *physically* demanding, even this can become laborious and toilsome. Writing (e.g., writing books, Bible studies, or devotionals) is another example of mental work that is at times a challenge, both mentally and spiritually. How can we ensure that our work (which is good) does not become toil (which is not good)? It all depends on our *attitude*. When I complain about having to do chores around the house, my wife is quick to help me adjust my attitude. She reminds me to be thankful that I am not stuck sitting somewhere bored to tears. At other times she tells me to be thankful that I can still walk and *do* some work! She gives wise counsel.

Thank the Lord for the work that you can still do as you grow old together. Don't allow a bad attitude to turn your work into laborious toil.

Discuss Together:
1. Discuss your attitude toward the work that you do regularly. Is it work or is it toil? Does your attitude need any "adjustment?"
2. Discuss some differences between work and toil. Specifically, where does the line cross between the two? Now consider your marriage. Discuss differences between work and toil in the chores you do for each other.
3. Discuss ways you can prevent your work from becoming toil, according to your response to the above question.
4. Re-read today's introductory scripture passage. Do you agree with Solomon's statement? Try to think of examples where this statement has proven to be true in your own life or in the life of another.
5. The gospel is about grace and forgiveness. Forgive each other for the times when your attitude toward work was, shall we say, less than commendable.

Study Together:
Study **Ecclesiastes 2**, which is an interesting commentary by King Solomon about work and its value. Discuss this passage together. What do you learn from it that you can apply to your daily life and specifically to your marriage? Ask the Lord to help you find enjoyment in your work and daily tasks, especially those that benefit your spouse. With the Lord's help, you will have the right attitude toward your work.

Pray Together:
Pray with your spouse and ask for the Lord's help to work without complaining and not to cross the line between work and toil.

37. Annoyance

<u>**Laugh Together**</u>:

Growing Old Together...

By John M. Cimbala, 2019

Ethel: (reading the paper) They did a survey and picked the most annoying word of the year.
Frank: What did they pick?
Ethel: The word "whatever."
Frank: Uh huh...Whatever...☺
Ethel: ☹...They should do a survey on the most annoying *husband*.
Frank: ☺ ...☹

Artwork by Helen Dickey

She followed Paul..., crying out, "These men are servants of the Most High God..." And this she kept doing for many days. Paul, having become greatly annoyed, turned and said to the spirit, "I command you in the name of Jesus Christ to come out of her."
Acts 16:17-18 (ESV)

<u>**Read Together**</u>:

Are you ever an *annoyance* to your spouse? The definition of **_annoyance_** is "an act or instance that leads to discontent, displeasure, irritation, or frustration; a nuisance." I sometimes cause my wife to feel the results described by this definition of annoyance. For example, I like humor and often make light of situations. While this in itself is not wrong, I sometimes continue this behavior to the point of *annoyance*. What I think is funny turns out to be annoying to my wife. *She* annoys *me* sometimes, too, by some of her comments or behaviors. The word "annoy" is not a common one in God's Word. In today's introductory scripture passage, however, we are told of an incident in which a servant girl kept trailing Paul and his companions, crying out about them. Her words were *true*, but after a few days of this, Paul became greatly annoyed. A demon or evil spirit in the girl was causing this annoyance, and Paul was able to drive it out in the name of Jesus Christ. This account reminds us that people can be annoyed, not only by silliness or half-truths, but also by true or even *prophetic* statements if they are repeated over and over. There is a time and place for humor, silliness, and repetition. However, when you realize that you are *annoying* your spouse, concentrate instead on saying and doing things that are helpful, encouraging, and appreciated.

Try not to annoy your spouse. Think of ways to approach conversations without causing annoyance. For example, always show *appreciation* to your spouse as you grow old together.

Discuss Together:
1. Name something your spouse does that is sometimes annoying. Discuss *why* this behavior annoys you.
2. Together, think of some specific actions you can take so that the annoyance discussed in the previous question can be avoided.
3. Where do you draw the line between silliness or humor and annoyance? Compare your answer to that of your spouse. Think of specific ways to bring your two lines closer together.
4. Re-read today's introductory scripture passage. It seems that Paul waited too long to do something about the annoyance he was feeling. How do *you* react to annoyance? For example, are you quick to become angry, or do you let it go on and on while inwardly seething? Discuss ways to lovingly let your spouse know when he or she is becoming annoying.
5. The gospel is about grace and forgiveness. Forgive each other for the times you have been annoying to each other.

Study Together:
Study **Luke 11:1-13**, which contains one of Jesus' parables about persistence and annoyance. Discuss what Jesus was trying to teach us through this parable. How does this parable connect to the Lord's Prayer given at the beginning of the chapter? With the Lord's help, you will be able to seek your spouse's help persistently yet not selfishly or annoyingly.

Pray Together:
Pray with your spouse and ask for the Lord's help in dealing with both sides of this issue: (1) becoming less annoying, and (2) reacting more appropriately when annoyed.

38. Appeasement

Laugh Together:

Growing Old Together...   By John M. Cimbala, 2019

Ethel: Do you ever agree with me just so I would stop talking?

Frank: Yes, dear.

Ethel: **Did you do it just *now*? !!**

Frank: Did I do *what* just now? ...☺ ... Is this some kind of trap?

Ethel: ☹...☹

Artwork by Helen Dickey

A king's wrath is a messenger of death, and a wise man will appease it.
Proverbs 16:14 (ESV)

Read Together:

Do you ever say something just to appease your spouse? The definition of **appeasement** is "to yield or concede in a conciliatory effort, sometimes at the expense of justice or the compromise of other principles; to pacify." This definition of appeasement has a *negative* connotation. But in today's introductory scripture passage, we are told that a wise man will appease the king's wrath, which sheds a much more *positive* light on the act of appeasing. In marriage, is appeasement good or bad? My wife often yields to my desires, and I sometimes yield to hers. I suppose this is a good kind of appeasement. Compromise is usually better, though. Actions toward our spouse that involve pacifying, yielding, or conceding are not necessarily sinful, and may even be loving. But there is one part of the above definition that we need to avoid when we appease, namely, when it is at the expense of justice or a compromise of our principles. This kind of appeasement *is* sinful. The Apostle Paul and his friends Barnabas and Titus did *not* compromise *their* principles when their freedom in Christ was attacked. In his letter to the Galatians, Paul says, *"Yet because of false brothers secretly brought in—who slipped in to spy out our freedom ...to them we did not yield in submission even for a moment, so that the truth of the gospel might be preserved for you."*

These men did not compromise the gospel in order to appease these false brothers.

When compromise is not working, It may be okay to appease your spouse as you grow old together. Be careful, however, not to compromise your *principles* when you do so.

Discuss Together:
1. Discuss the difference between appeasement and compromise of principles. How do you distinguish between the two?
2. Which of you is more likely to appease the other? When you do so, is it done with the motivation of love?
3. Think back to a time in your marriage where appeasement rather than compromise occurred, but this action involved a compromise of principles. How did it make you feel? Discuss how the situation could have been handled differently.
4. Think of a recurring situation in your marriage in which you "yield or concede in a conciliatory effort" (as per our definition of appeasement). How did it make you feel? Has too much appeasement lead to suppressed resentful feelings?
5. The gospel is about grace and forgiveness. Forgive each other for times when you appeased your spouse with an attitude that could have been more loving. Also, forgive each other for times you compromised your principles just to keep the peace.

Study Together:
Study **Acts 16:16-30**, which describes the arrest and imprisonment of Paul and Silas. This portion of scripture deals with many issues related to today's devotional, such as annoyance, unfair treatment, concession, appeasement, and compromise. Discuss how Paul and Silas dealt with these issues and whether they ever compromised their Christian principles. With the Lord's help, you will be given the strength and wisdom to handle difficult situations in your life.

Pray Together:
Pray with your spouse and ask for the Lord's help in conceding or appeasing to him or her when appropriate, without compromising your principles.

39. Honesty

Growing Old Together...

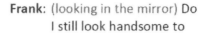 By John M. Cimbala, 2019

Frank: (looking in the mirror) Do I still look handsome to you?

Ethel: (takes off her glasses) Yes, you look *very* handsome to me! ☺

Frank: ... ☺

Ethel: ☺

Frank: ☺...☹

Artwork by Helen Dickey

One who is faithful in a very little is also faithful in much, and one who is dishonest in a very little is also dishonest in much.
Luke 16:10 (ESV)

Read Together:

Is it ever acceptable to be dishonest with your spouse? The definition of **honesty** is "truthfulness, sincerity, or frankness; without deceit or fraud." Dishonesty is thus the *opposite*, implying deceit, fraud, or insincerity. Hopefully none of us is ever dishonest about important matters. But is it okay to tell "little white lies" about *unimportant* matters? For example, is it okay to tell my wife that the new recipe she had raved about did not taste nearly as good as it looked? In today's introductory scripture passage, Jesus reminds us that dishonesty in inconsequential matters often leads to dishonesty in matters of greater consequence. My wife and I have vowed to be completely honest with each other, even if it hurts. To avoid hurt feelings, however, I sometimes say nothing or try to change the subject when I am, as the saying goes, between a rock and a hard place – when saying the truth would hurt but lying would violate her trust. Sometimes it is possible to couch comments so that they are both truthful and emotionally pain free, but I usually can't get away with trying to avoid an honest answer. My wife is clever enough to realize when she has put me in an awkward situation. After years of marriage, we both realize that dishonesty is never a good option, even in minor things. So, I lovingly share my truthful thoughts or opinions, respect her reaction, empathize with her, and move on. My wife reciprocates, and this mutual respect and honesty strengthens our marriage.

As you grow old together, maintain heartfelt honesty with your spouse.

Discuss Together:
1. Discuss the dividing line between "little white lies" and dishonesty. Is it ever okay to be untruthful to your spouse, even in little things? What about surprise parties or things of that nature? Think of ways to respond, or not respond, while preserving truthfulness – to reveal secrets without lying.
2. Reflect upon a situation you have already admitted and discussed together, in which you were dishonest with your spouse. How did you justify your actions at the time? Do you feel the same about this mistruth now as you did then? Explain your thoughts and feelings.
3. Looking back at the situation of the previous question, discuss how you could (or *should*) have handled it differently, that is, without being dishonest.
4. Think back to a situation in which you *were* completely honest with your spouse but this honesty hurt his or her feelings. Looking back, how could you have addressed the situation in an honest fashion while still preserving your spouse's feelings?
5. The gospel is about grace and forgiveness. Forgive each other for the times when you have not been entirely truthful with your spouse.

Study Together:
Study **Luke 16:1-13**, which recounts Jesus' parable of the dishonest manager. This particular parable is one of the hardest to understood because it seems to imply God's approval of dishonesty in business transactions. Discuss ways to interpret this parable that do not condone dishonesty. How could the servant have handled the situation differently, trusting in God? With the Lord's help, you will be honest with others, and especially with your spouse, in all circumstances.

Pray Together:
Pray with your spouse and ask the Lord to help you be honest in a way that preserves not only personal integrity but also your spouse's feelings.

40. Deceitfulness

Laugh Together:

Growing Old Together...   By John M. Cimbala, 2019

Ethel: (looking in cupboard) Did you put this dish in the wrong place ***on purpose*** just so I wouldn't ask you to put dishes away again?

Frank: Uhh...You look pretty tonight, dear. ☺

Ethel: You can't flatter your way out of this one, ***dear***...☹.

Frank: You look *very* pretty tonight, dear. ☺

Ethel: ☹

Artwork by Helen Dickey

The heart is deceitful above all things, and desperately sick; who can understand it?
Jeremiah 17:9 (ESV)

Read Together:

Have you ever been deceitful with your spouse? The definition of **deceitfulness** is "being or acting in a way that is untrustworthy, two-faced, misleading, or fraudulent." Deceitfulness can be more destructive than dishonesty, especially in marriage. It is wrong to lie to your spouse. But it is *deplorable* to deliberately *deceive* him or her. As the above definition implies, deceitfulness involves purposely misleading and/or intentionally hiding something from someone. Jeremiah tells us in today's introductory scripture passage that the heart is deceitful above all things! It is frightening to think that such wickedness resides deep within us. How can we avoid being deceitful? In 1 Peter 2:1, the Apostle Peter instructs believers to *"put away all malice and all deceit and hypocrisy and envy and all slander."* Peter reminds us that these harmful acts should never be perpetrated by a follower of Christ, even toward strangers. How much more so does this reminder apply toward our *spouse,* our life partner and closest friend! How can we hope to control such a deceitful heart? The Apostle Paul gives us the answer in Romans 7:23-25: *"...I see in my members another law waging war against the law of my mind and* *making me captive to the law of sin that dwells in my members. Wretched man that I am! Who will deliver me from this body of death? Thanks be to God through Jesus Christ our Lord!"* In other words, it is only through the grace of Jesus Christ and the conviction of the Holy Spirit that we can keep from being deceitful.

As you grow old together, never let any deceitfulness be found in you, *especially* deceitfulness toward your spouse.

Discuss Together:
1. Discuss the similarities and differences between dishonesty and deceitfulness. Which is more harmful? Why?
2. Is it ever okay to be deceitful? Discuss why or why not.
3. Think back to a situation in which you were deceitful with your spouse, preferably one that you have already admitted and discussed together. (If you cannot recall being deceitful with your spouse, discuss an act of deceitfulness toward someone *else*.) How did you justify your actions at the time? As you reflect, from a position of time and distance, on this deceitful action, how do you feel about it now?
4. While reflecting upon the situation of the previous question, discuss how you could (or *should*) have handled it differently, that is, to avoid being deceitful.
5. The gospel is about grace and forgiveness. If painful recollections and fears have surfaced as a result of this devotional, openly share these feelings. Then forgive each other for the times when deceitfulness reared its ugly head in your lives together as a couple.

Study Together:
Study **1 Samuel 27-29**, which describes how David fled to the Philistines to escape from King Saul's pursuit. Read how David deceived King Achish, yet how Achish trusted David. Discuss how you feel about David's deceitfulness and about how he could have handled it differently, trusting in God. With the Lord's help, you will not be deceitful with others, and especially with your spouse, in all future circumstances.

Pray Together:
Pray with your spouse and ask for the Lord's help to, as Peter writes, *"put away all malice and all deceit and hypocrisy and envy and all slander."*

41. Concern

Laugh Together:

Growing Old Together...

By John M. Cimbala, 2019

Frank: (hungry) Can you make me some breakfast?

Ethel: (not feeling well) I don't think so. I'm so sick I feel like I'm going to die.

Frank: Can you wait to die till *after* you make me some breakfast? ☺

Ethel: ...☹

Artwork by Helen Dickey

For I have no one like him, who will be genuinely concerned for your welfare. For they all seek their own interests, not those of Jesus Christ. But you know Timothy's proven worth, how as a son with a father he has served with me in the gospel.

Philippians 2:20-22 (ESV)

Read Together:

Are you genuinely concerned about your spouse and his or her needs? The definition of **concern** is "to consider the needs and difficulties of others and take an active interest in their feelings, capabilities, and perspectives in order to assist them with the difficulties they face and act with integrity and warmth." The natural human tendency, a result of the Fall, is to be selfish and not show deep concern about others' needs. This unattractive trait is frequently most pronounced in relationship to a spouse. Perhaps I have become so used to my wife, and all that she willingly offers, that I take her for granted. What I *should* do, however, is be like Paul's friend Timothy in today's introductory scripture passage. Timothy was genuinely concerned about the people in Philippi. Paul goes on to describe how most people seek their own interests, but Timothy sought what was best for others, including Paul and the Philippian believers. Likewise, God's plan for my wife and myself is for *me* to be, as Philippians 2:20 suggests, genuinely concerned about *her* welfare more than that of myself or anyone else. Doing so takes thoughtful effort. I must consciously endeavor to show concern. I am not talking about *fake* concern, which my wife easily spots; I mean *genuine* concern. I have to be empathetic to her situation/circumstance and actively think about how I can best help her. For me, this is not so easily accomplished (and may be a struggle for you as well). Jesus coined the famous "Golden Rule," recorded in the seventh chapter of Matthew: *"Do to others what you would have them do to you."* This is great advice for *all* relationships, and especially for marriage relationships.

Determine to stay genuinely concerned about the needs of your spouse as you grow old together.

Discuss Together:
1. Do you sometimes find it difficult to show genuine concern for your spouse? Discuss possible reasons as to why.
2. Discuss how God has revealed his concern for you. Having been made in his image, how can we imitate this attribute?
3. Discuss specific ways in which you and your spouse can improve your ability to show genuine concern for each other. Practice these ideas in the coming weeks and gently remind each other when you fail.
4. Think of a friend or family member who has (or had, in the case of someone deceased) consistent and genuine concern for you. Discuss how it made you feel and how you might imitate that person in showing concern for others.
5. The gospel is about grace and forgiveness. Forgive each other for the times you thought of yourself ahead of your spouse and did not show concern for his or her needs and feelings.

Study Together:
Study **Philippians 2**, where the Apostle Paul provides examples of people who showed true concern for others, including Timothy, Epaphroditus, Paul himself, and Jesus Christ. Discuss how each of these individuals showed genuine concern. Discuss the extent to which Christ showed concern for us. With the Lord's help, you will also imitate Christ.

Pray Together:
Pray with your spouse and ask for the Lord's help in showing genuine concern for each other.

42. Servanthood

Growing Old Together...   By John M. Cimbala, 2019

Ethel: (frustrated) I'm tired of waiting on you hand and foot.
Frank: Well, that's better than waiting on me with *both* hands and *both* feet! ...☺
Ethel: ☺...☹
Frank: ☺

Artwork by Helen Dickey

It shall not be so among you. But whoever would be great among you must be your servant.
Matthew 20:26 (ESV)

Read Together:

Do you sometimes feel like a *servant* to your spouse? There are many definitions of *servant*, most of which deal with employment by or bondage to another person. The most appropriate definition of **servant** here, though, is "a devoted and helpful follower or supporter; a helper." In the New Testament, servanthood is not something to fear or of which to be ashamed. Rather, Jesus spoke on several occasions about how we should *voluntarily* be servants – he encourages servanthood! In today's introductory scripture passage, Jesus claims that to be great you must be a servant. How is this possible since it seems so contradictory? We find the answer in the next two verses; Jesus goes on to say, "*...whoever would be first among you must be your slave, even as the Son of Man came not to be served but to serve, and to give his life as a ransom for many.*" We see that Christ himself, though he was God and Master, knew that his purpose on earth was *to serve* rather than to *be served*. And this he did *voluntarily*, even to the point of dying for those he served. We must try to have this same attitude of servanthood in our marriages. When my wife tells me to do something, I sometimes try to be funny and quip, "Do I look like a servant?" Her answer is always, "Yes." She then reminds me of what Jesus said about being a servant. We both need to be devoted supporters and helpers of each other; continually striving for a servant's attitude. I am learning that a conscientious effort toward remembering and *applying* that goal, though not easy or natural, works best in our marriage.

Considering that Jesus came not to be served but to serve, strive to always be a willing servant to your spouse as you grow old together.

Discuss Together:
1. Jesus tells us in today's introductory scripture passage that in order to be great, you must be a servant. This goes against natural logic! Explain Jesus' statement and how it can be applied.
2. Do you have a servant's heart? *Should* you? Discuss ways to turn a selfish heart into a servant's heart.
3. Discuss why an attitude of servanthood is especially important in the context of the marriage relationship. List some practical ways in which you and your spouse can better and more willingly serve each other.
4. Re-read aloud the definition of servant provided above. Do you show these qualities of servanthood toward your spouse? Lovingly point out situations in which your spouse can become a better servant. Ask for compassionate feedback on how you can be a more effective supporter and helper to your spouse.
5. The gospel is about grace and forgiveness. Forgive each other for times when you chose to be served rather than to serve your spouse.

Study Together:
Study **Matthew 25:14-30**, which is Jesus' parable of the talents. Discuss the difference in attitude between the first two servants and the third servant. Particularly notable here is that the master, on his return, settled accounts with each of them; the servants did not even get to keep any of the gain from their investments! With the Lord's help, you, like those first two servants, will always have a servant's attitude toward others, especially toward your spouse.

Pray Together:
Pray with your spouse and ask for the Lord's help in maintaining a servant's attitude.

43. Pomposity

Laugh Together:

Growing Old Together...

By John M. Cimbala, 2019

Frank: (after turning 60) I can't believe I am **60 years old** already!

Ethel: Yes, but you don't look a day over 50! ☺

Frank: ☺ ...♥ Thanks. How old *do* I look?

Ethel: You look *ten years* over 50! ☺

Frank: ...☺ ...☹

Artwork by Helen Dickey

For by the grace given to me I say to everyone among you not to think of himself more highly than he ought to think.
Romans 12:3 (ESV)

Read Together:

Do you think highly of yourself? Do you think of yourself as important and/or good-looking and therefore expect others to take special note of you? If so, this is called pomposity; you are being pompous. The definition of **pompous** is "having or exhibiting self-importance; pretentious; haughty; overtly prideful." The Bible is filled with condemnations about this kind of attitude. For example, Paul warns in today's introductory scripture passage against pomposity. He tells us not to think more highly of ourselves than we ought. And *how* ought we to think of ourselves? Paul says to think of ourselves with "sober judgment" (in other words, *realistically*). As we age, our appearance matures as well. Youthful beauty is replaced by seasoned attractiveness. Our memories, strength, and abilities wane. This certainly helps us have more sober judgment! Yet it is possible to remain pompous in spite of the ongoing changes wrought to our temporal selves. For example, I tend to think of myself as younger than I really am, and I subconsciously expect others to see me in that same way. A recent high school reunion abruptly changed this attitude, however. Everyone looked so old! I realized that I probably looked equally as old to them! It was definitely a humbling experience. As we grow older, marriage has the potential of naturally tempering pomposity. I am glad that my wife and I are close in age so that we can grow old together gracefully, without being pompous.

Don't think too highly of yourself as you grow old together. Instead, be thankful for the grace God has given you.

Discuss Together:
1. Re-read today's introductory scripture passage from Romans. Discuss why the Apostle Paul warns us not to think too highly of ourselves.
2. The word "pomposity" is probably not in your daily vocabulary. Now that you know what it means, think of someone you know (or a celebrity, politician, etc.) who is pompous. Discuss how this person's pomposity affects your opinion of him or her.
3. Look again at today's comic. Have you ever been sobered, like Frank, after being pompous? Discuss when and where this event took place. How did it make you feel?
4. Read Galatians 3:28, which reminds us that we are all one in Christ Jesus; there is no difference between male and female in matters of faith and salvation. With this in mind, discuss why pomposity should never enter a Christian marriage.
5. The gospel is about grace and forgiveness. Forgive each other for those times when excessive pride, a haughty spirit, or pomposity replaced sober judgment in your marriage.

Study Together:
Study **Luke 14:7-11**, which is Jesus' parable warning people not to take a place of honor at a feast unless specifically invited to do so. In this parable, the pompous person who presumes to be a guest of honor is humiliated when asked to give up his seat to someone more important. He ends up sitting in the *lowest* place! Discuss this parable with each other. What lessons from this parable can be applied to your marriage? With the Lord's help, you will have enough wisdom to avoid being humiliated like the man in this parable.

Pray Together:
Pray with your spouse and ask for the Lord's help as we strive to think of ourselves with "sober judgment" rather than with pomposity.

44. Frustration

:

Growing Old Together...

By John M. Cimbala, 2019

Frank: (coming home, empty handed) Honey, I'm home!
Ethel: Where's the milk? Did you forget to stop to get milk like I asked you?
Frank: Umm...Maybe...Oops...☺
Ethel: ☹
Frank: You look so pretty when you're angry.
Ethel: Then I must be getting *really* pretty right now! ☹

Artwork by Helen Dickey

Without consultation, plans are frustrated,
But with many counselors they succeed.
Proverbs 15:22 (NASV)

Read Together:

How often do you frustrate or get frustrated with your spouse? Today's comic hits home because, like Ethel, we have probably all experienced this kind of frustration. One definition of ***frustration*** is "a feeling of dissatisfaction resulting from unfulfilled needs or unresolved problems." I have to admit that *I* frustrate my wife much more than *she* frustrates me! Most of her frustration occurs when I am not actively listening as she speaks. Then I end up buying the wrong thing, forgetting to do something, repeating myself, etc. When you let reasonable requests go unheeded (especially your spouse's), you provoke frustration in the requestor. While not necessarily *sinful*, an attitude of frustration is *negative*. If one spouse frustrates the other *intentionally*, however, this *is* sinful and should spur repentance. **Psalm 33:10** gives a *positive* spin on frustration: "*The Lord ... frustrates the plans of the peoples.*" In other words, God is in control and prevents us from doing anything that goes against his sovereign will, regardless of how hard we try. This act of frustration, since it comes from God himself, is *not* sinful and agrees with an alternative definition of frustration, "prevention from progressing,

92

succeeding, or being fulfilled." I take great comfort knowing that God frustrates the plans of the peoples. I would rather the outcome be in God's hands than in the hands of others (including mine).

As you grow old together, try not to frustrate your spouse. And, when you feel frustration growing within, be kind and gracious in your response. In most cases, your spouse has not acted with ill intent.

Discuss Together:
1. Discuss situations in which frustration, while not necessarily sinful, can *turn* sinful.
2. What is the opposite of frustration? Discuss how to steer your conversations and actions away from frustration and toward the opposite of frustration.
3. Take turns mentioning something that your spouse says or does that frustrates you. Discuss specific ways to avoid frustrating your spouse in these areas. Keep in mind that the purpose of this activity is to improve your relationship, not to rebuke each other harshly.
4. How do you respond to frustration in your marriage? Ignore it? Talk it out? Retaliate? React in anger? Let it fester? Calmly walk away? Discuss how you and your spouse *should* respond to frustration and how you can improve in this area.
5. The gospel is about grace and forgiveness. Forgive each other for those times when you have purposely frustrated your spouse.

Study Together:
Study **Proverbs 21:9**, **21:19**, and **25:24**, which are somewhat comical sayings about living with a quarrelsome wife. Solomon collected and compiled proverbs and sayings from many sources, so it is uncertain if he wrote all of these himself. What *is* known, however, is that the author was frustrated with his wife's attitude and constant bickering to the point that he would rather live on the roof or in a desert than with his wife! Discuss how, with the Lord's help, you can avoid this extreme kind of frustration.

Pray Together:
Pray with your spouse and ask for the Lord's help in avoiding frustration – on both the giving and receiving ends.

45. Vanity

Laugh Together:

Growing Old Together...

By John M. Cimbala, 2019

Frank: Neil dyed his hair and he looks *so* much younger now.
Ethel: That's nice.
Frank: Should I dye *my* hair?
Ethel: ...Neil **has** hair ...☺
Frank: ...☺ ...☹
Ethel: ☺

Artwork by Helen Dickey

Behold, all of you have seen it yourselves; why then have you become altogether vain?
Job 27:12 (ESV)

Read Together:
There are two primary definitions of the word vanity. One is a synonym of futility or banality as discussed elsewhere in this devotional. The definition of **vanity** under consideration *here*, however, is "excessive pride in or esteem of one's own appearance or achievements; self-admiration." There are many passages in the Bible that use the word vanity or vain as in the *first* definition, but I found only one where the *second* definition is implied. In today's introductory scripture passage, Job is defending himself against his (unhelpful) friends' accusations, mockingly suggesting that they are so vain because they think they know everything. This kind of vanity or self-admiration has no place in a Christian's life, especially in marriage. We are not to be vain about abilities or physical attributes that exceed those of our spouse. Likewise, we should not be jealous of the attributes of our spouse that exceed our own. God designed and created male and female to be *complementary* to each other; where one lacks, the other typically excels. This is especially important (and *necessary*) as we age. As I ponder this, I realize that the two primary definitions of vanity are actually related. Excessive pride or

self-admiration is futile, pointless, and ineffectual. In other words, vanity is vanity!

As you grow old together, your physical prowess and attractiveness begin to ebb. In natural order then, reasons for feelings of vanity start to diminish as well. Be careful, however, not to be critical of your spouse; instead, build each other up and emphasize each other's good qualities and character.

Discuss Together:

1. Consider the statement "vanity is vanity." Do you agree with this statement? Discuss how this might apply to your marriage.
2. Has vanity ever been an issue in your marriage? If so, discuss how and when. Then forgive each other and discuss ways to prevent feelings of vanity before this issue becomes problematic.
3. Take turns complimenting each other about qualities or abilities that are more prominent in your spouse than in yourself. In this way, enjoy building each other up. Ensure, however, that these compliments are not only genuine, but also do not lead to vanity.
4. Discuss where the line is drawn between feeling good about yourself and vanity. Then come up with practical ways to help each other avoid crossing that line.
5. The gospel is about grace and forgiveness. Forgive each other for past expressions of vanity that were hurtful.

Study Together:

Study **Genesis 4:17-24**, which has some hidden gems – lessons to be found within the genealogies at which most people give only a cursory glance. The man Lamech in this passage apparently had an above average quota of vanity! Discuss what we learn about Lamech from this reading, especially concerning his two wives and how he treated them. Then discuss what Lamech could have (*should* have) done differently. With the Lord's help, love, gentleness, forgiveness, and servanthood will triumph over vanity in your marriage as you grow old together.

Pray Together:

Pray with your spouse and ask for the Lord's help in striving to do your best without becoming vain.

46. Disillusionment

<u>**Laugh Together**</u>:

Growing Old Together...   By John M. Cimbala, 2019

Ethel: (Frank comes home from dentist) How did your teeth cleaning go?

Frank: Stephanie said my newly whitened teeth make me look 10 years younger! ☺

Ethel: Uh huh.

Frank: What do *you* think? ♥

Ethel: I think Stephanie has a good sense of humor. ☺

Frank: ...☺

Artwork by Helen Dickey

Not that we are sufficient in ourselves to claim anything as coming from us, but our sufficiency is from God, who has made us sufficient to be ministers of a new covenant, not of the letter but of the Spirit.
2 Corinthians 3:5-6a (ESV)

<u>**Read Together**</u>:

We feel disillusioned when our confidence is shattered, and confidence is easily shattered when we base it on ourselves. The definition of **disillusionment** is "a feeling of disappointment resulting from the discovery that something is not as good as one believed it to be; disenchanted." In today's introductory scripture passage, the Apostle Paul reminds us that our sufficiency comes not from ourselves, but from God. How does this scripture passage apply to *marriage*? Disillusionment can come from something related to *yourself*, or from something related to your *spouse*. For example, I am somewhat like Frank in today's comic and think I look younger than I actually am. I have this mental image of what I looked like ten years ago and want others to see me that way. But a video, a picture, or even a glance in the mirror quickly crashes me back to reality; I then feel disillusioned. Here are some other common examples. Husbands may expect their wives to respond to their affection like when they were young. Wives may expect their husbands to treat them romantically like when they were dating. Both husband and wife often end up disillusioned by a cold dose of reality; time takes its toll on our bodies and minds. But don't be let yourselves become disillusioned by temporal things; God is your confidence. He has made you sufficient and will ensure that your *souls* remain healthy and secure through the grace of Jesus Christ, who gives us a real and lasting hope that never fails!

How can you avoid disillusionment as you grow old together? Continue to love and respect each other, maintaining communication through the inevitable changes.

Discuss Together:
1. Re-read the definition of disillusionment given above. Then discuss some instances where you have become disillusioned (not necessarily regarding your marriage). How did those instances make you feel?
2. Discuss potential ways you could have avoided feeling disillusioned or handled things differently in the instances of the previous question.
3. Think back to when you were engaged and had romantic visions of your marriage. Do you now realize you feel disillusioned by any of those visions as time has marched on in your marriage? Discuss your feelings lovingly and gently with your spouse.
4. Turn the previous question around and think of some things about your spouse that actually turned out better than you expected! Encourage each other with these acknowledgments.
5. The gospel is about grace and forgiveness. Forgive each other for the times you expected more from your spouse than you actually received. Thank the Lord for the times you received more from your spouse than you expected.

Study Together:
Study **1 Samuel 17**, which is the familiar account of David and Goliath. Discuss on what Saul, David, and Goliath based their confidence. Which of their sources of confidence were appropriate, and which were not? On what are you and your spouse basing your confidence? Do you think that your sources of confidence will bring disillusionment or sufficiency?

Pray Together:
Remember that your sufficiency comes not from yourselves but from God. Pray with your spouse and ask for the Lord's help in prioritizing and keeping things in proper perspective as you grow old together.

47. Ignoring

Growing Old Together...   By John M. Cimbala, 2019

Ethel: Do you remember when I was talking to June a few weeks ago?
Frank: Yes.
Ethel: Do you remember what we *said*?
Frank: No. I don't hear well when there is too much estrogen around.
Ethel: ...☺ ...☹
Frank: ☺

Artwork by Helen Dickey

Whoever ignores instruction despises himself, but he who listens to reproof gains intelligence.
Proverbs 15:32 (ESV)

Read Together:

Do you sometimes ignore your spouse? I do. The definition of **ignore** is "to refuse to take notice of or acknowledge; to disregard intentionally." That is a deeply convicting definition, especially the word *intentionally*. I have mentioned elsewhere in this book that I sometimes (*intentionally*) ignore my wife, especially when she talks on and on about something that does not interest me or involve me. In such times, I often interrupt, "What is your point?" hoping that she will summarize and get to the end. Sometimes I ask, "Why are you telling me this, and what does it have to do with me?" This does not usually go over well. What I should realize is that sometimes she just wants to *talk*, even if the topic is not important. I, on the other hand, tend to talk only when necessary (why waste my voice?). This habit of ignoring my wife is normally not too damaging from *my* viewpoint, perhaps not from *hers*. But sometimes she tells me important things or tries to correct me; if I ignore her in such cases, I sin against her and am convicted. In today's introductory scripture passage, Solomon warns his readers against ignoring instruction and that doing so actually involves a kind of self-despising. The last part of the verse is more positive. Applying it to marriage, we "gain intelligence" (learn something useful) by listening to and not ignoring our spouse.

Don't ignore your spouse as you grow old together. Cherish the times you talk together, even about unimportant topics. The day may come when one of you is unable to speak, and talking together will be missed.

Discuss Together:
1. Discuss potential damage to relationships caused by ignoring, which includes saying, "I'll get back to you on that," and then *not* doing so.
2. Do you set aside certain times of day for talking to your spouse? For example, while walking together, eating meals, or just sitting on the couch with the TV *off*? If so, discuss whether the time you set aside is adequate and consider adding more time. If not, consider scheduling some daily time to simply *talk* to each other (about things concerning only the two of you) to encourage better communication.
3. Read again the above definition of *ignore*. Discuss situations when you are most likely to intentionally ignore your spouse, perhaps right before bed, while working on meals, when the football game is on... To better respect your spouse, agree not to discuss important matters during those times so that neither of you feels "put off" or rejected.
4. In today's introductory scripture passage, Solomon implies that ignoring someone (e.g., your spouse) involves despising *yourself*. Do you agree? Discuss the impact of this proverb on your relationship.
5. The gospel is about grace and forgiveness. Forgive each other for the times you have intentionally ignored your spouse.

Study Together:
Study **Matthew 12:1-14**, the account about Jesus claiming to be Lord of the Sabbath and the Pharisees reacting to his claim. It always amazes me that even after the Pharisees see Jesus heal someone right in front of their eyes, they go out and plot how they might kill him! (V. 13-14). Discuss what the Pharisees *ignored* about Jesus and his teachings. With the Lord's help, you will be given an increased desire to not ignore others (especially your spouse!) and so despise yourself.

Pray Together:
Pray with your spouse and ask for the Lord's help in carefully listening rather than ignoring him or her.

48. Thankfulness

Laugh Together:

Growing Old Together... By John M. Cimbala, 2019

Frank: (angry) **Ugh!** You burnt my toast!

Ethel: Be thankful you *have* toast.

Frank: (muttering) *Other* wives don't burn *their* husbands' toast.

Ethel: **What did you say?** ...☹

Frank: Umm ...☺...*Other* wives don't make *their* husbands' toast...☺ ... (sweating) Thank you for making me toast. ☺

Ethel: ...☺

Artwork by Helen Dickey

I give thanks to my God always for you because of the grace of God that was given you in Christ Jesus.
1 Corinthians 1:4 (ESV)

Read Together:

Are you always thankful for your spouse? The definition of **thankfulness** is "a feeling of gratitude and appreciation; gratefulness." I certainly appreciate the many things my wife does for me, and I am grateful that she is faithful and loves me even when I don't deserve it. However, I cannot claim to *always* be thankful, and I certainly do not *express* my thankfulness often enough. In today's introductory scripture passage, Paul tells the readers of his letter that he *always* thanks God for them. What? How is that possible? I think Paul is talking about an *attitude* of thankfulness, which can be present even without verbalizing it. But we need to do *both*: have an attitude of thankfulness *and* express it. In the past year, a divorced friend convicted me to thank God each day for the wife he gave me. That was good advice! So now, when my wife and I pray together each morning, I try to remember to thank the Lord for the gift of my wife, and I find that the expression of thankfulness *in spoken prayer* has a way of solidifying that thankfulness. Even on days when I am not feeling especially thankful, like after an argument, giving thanks during our prayer time can change my attitude, making the thankfulness more genuine.

Always be thankful for your spouse as you grow old together. Remember that marriage was designed by God for your mutual benefit.

Discuss Together:
1. Discuss some things about your spouse for which you are thankful. Express your thankfulness verbally to each other.
2. Discuss times or situations when you feel most appreciated by your spouse – when your spouse shows sincere thankfulness, either in attitude or in verbal expression.
3. In today's introductory scripture passage, Paul claims that he is *always* thankful. Discuss how to always be thankful for your spouse. List some ways to encourage thankfulness of each other as you grow old together.
4. Discuss what a lack of thankfulness may indicate about a person. Pride? Greed? Selfishness? Frailty? Unconfessed sin? A sinful heart?
5. The gospel is about grace and forgiveness. What aspects of the gospel involve thankfulness? Forgive each other for times you have taken your spouse for granted and were not thankful for the wonderful gift God has given you.

Study Together:
Study **Colossians 3:12-17**, where the Apostle Paul instructs Christians how to treat each other. List the behaviors or attitudes that he encourages us to practice or "put on." How many times in this short passage does Paul mention *thankfulness*? Discuss how an attitude of thankfulness can be a kind of catalyst for the other attributes in this list. Re-read the passage with your spouse in mind. With the Lord's help, you will have an attitude of thankfulness for the spouse he has given you to love and enjoy throughout your life.

Pray Together:
Pray with your spouse and ask for the Lord's help in showing more thankfulness, especially verbally, for him or her.

49. Acceptance

Laugh Together:

Growing Old Together...

By John M. Cimbala, 2019

Ethel: I don't like how they call these our "Golden Years." They are *not* golden!

Frank: Actually it's more like our *"Metallic Years."*

Ethel: What do you mean?

Frank: Gold in our teeth, silver in our hair, titanium in our hips...

Ethel: ☺...I guess "Golden Years" isn't so bad!

Artwork by Helen Dickey

I appeal to you... to present your bodies as a living sacrifice, holy and acceptable to God, which is your spiritual worship.
Romans 12:1 (ESV)

Read Together:

Have you fully come to terms with growing old? In other words, have you accepted the fact that you are no longer young and many aspects of your body are beginning to decline? The definition of ***acceptance*** is "the action or process of consenting to something as being adequate; approval." I would not necessarily say that I *approve* of getting old and all the physical changes that go with it. On the other hand, there is not a lot I can do about it, so I must *accept* my aging and thank God for having given me a long life. Some people have trouble accepting their aging, and maybe even more so that of their spouse! I imagine my wife does not like to see less hair on my head, more wrinkles around my eyes, and more flab at my neck... She, like myself, is experiencing changes (which I won't mention here). The old saying is, "accept someone, warts and all." In our case, we don't have many warts, but we are getting a lot of age spots and skin tags! Fortunately, my wife and I have learned to accept these changes in our bodies, realizing that most of them are beyond our control anyway. In today's introductory scripture passage, Paul reminds us that our bodies are living sacrifices that we must present to God, and God receives us with acceptance. That is great news, especially as we age!

You are acceptable to God. Your spouse is acceptable to God. You made a covenant to stay together until death parts you. Therefore, you have no choice but to accept each other, warts and all, age spots and all, as you grow old together.

Discuss Together:
1. In today's introductory scripture passage, the Apostle Paul tells us to present our bodies as a living sacrifice, holy and acceptable to God. He then says that this is your spiritual worship. Discuss what he means. What do our bodies have to do with worship?
2. Discuss some aspects of aging that you find hard to accept. Why? What makes these particular aspects so hard? Think of some practical ways to encourage your spouse to accept the aspects of aging that he or she mentioned.
3. Look again at today's comic. Discuss how humor can help us be more accepting of the trials that life throws at us.
4. Discuss practical ways to develop a more accepting attitude toward your bodies as you grow old together. However, be cautious of letting this acceptance lead to complacency. We should always strive to keep our physical bodies as healthy as possible, especially as we age.
5. The gospel is about grace and forgiveness. Forgive each other for the times when you have not readily accepted the trials of aging that you and your spouse have been given.

Study Together:
Study **Ecclesiastes 5:8-20.** A cursory reading of this passage may be depressing. A closer look, however, reveals hidden gems in this commentary about life written by King Solomon, the wisest man who ever lived. In particular, study the last few verses. Discuss how Solomon encourages us to accept our "few days" as a gift of God. Also, discuss how God keeps us occupied with joy in our hearts. Discuss how to apply these principles to your marriage and pray for the Lord's help in doing so.

Pray Together:
Pray with your spouse and ask for the Lord's help in having an attitude of acceptance. Promise to help each other accept the changes, especially those that are beyond your control.

50. Pretension

Laugh Together:

Growing Old Together...

By John M. Cimbala, 2019

Frank: I can't believe we're turning 60. Don't I look *younger* than that?

Ethel: Yep. You look **10 years younger**!

Frank: ☺... Really? ...☺...♥...☺

Ethel: Yep. You look **10 years younger than 70**! ☺

Frank: ...☺ ...☹

Ethel: ☺

Artwork by Helen Dickey

Beware of the scribes... who devour widows' houses and for a pretense make long prayers. They will receive the greater condemnation.
Luke 20:46-47 (ESV)

Read Together:

Are you ever pretentious? The definition of ***pretension*** is "a claim made, indirectly or by implication, to some (often false) quality or merit; an assertion intended to impress." Today's comic makes light of pretension in our *looks* as we age. If you have been married for a long time, it is quite difficult to be pretentious with your spouse; he or she knows you too well! We sometimes fool ourselves, believing we look younger or thinner than we actually are. This mild form of pretentiousness, as long as it remains playful, is not harmful. In today's introductory scripture passage, however, Jesus points to a much more *dangerous* type of pretension. The Jewish religious leaders were hypocritical and often chastised by Jesus for it. In today's introductory scripture passage, he condemns their long pretentious prayers. They did not pray earnestly from their hearts for God's forgiveness or to worship him, but rather they prayed so that others would hear and be impressed. How sad. What about us? It is natural to want others to think highly of us, and it is not sinful to offer long prayers, but we must be careful of our motives. We must not let ourselves become pretentious in any aspect of our Christian lives, as this would not be honoring our God and Savior. For example, I enjoy memorizing scripture. This comes in handy at Bible studies, yet it is tempting to spout off scripture verses just to show everyone that I know them by heart. When I catch myself doing this, I think of the above scripture passage; I am being pretentious.

Ask the Holy Spirit to prevent the slide into pretentious behavior in regards to your looks or anything else as you grow old together.

Discuss Together:
1. Think of some situations in your marriage in which you are tempted to be pretentious. Discuss practical ways to avoid being pretentious with each other when so tempted.
2. Discuss some instances or circumstances when you have *been* pretentious with your spouse or vice versa. How did it make you and your spouse feel? How should you or your spouse have handled the situation differently?
3. What are some antonyms for *pretentiousness*? Discuss practical ways to display *these* character traits rather than the ungodly trait of pretentiousness.
4. Read today's introductory scripture passage again. There is a warning at the end: pretentious people will receive greater condemnation. Discuss why you think Jesus said this and how it applies to you, especially in matters related to your marriage.
5. The gospel is about grace and forgiveness. Forgive each other for the times you have been pretentious with your spouse.

Study Together:
Study **Acts 8:9-24**, which is the account of Simon, the sorcerer. It seems that Simon's entire life was pretentious. He tricked people with magic and then boasted that he was someone great. When Peter and John laid their hands on people to receive the Holy Spirit, Simon offered them money for the ability to do likewise! Discuss Peter's response to Simon's pretension. When you are tempted to be pretentious, remember Simon and instead be genuine, modest, and humble.

Pray Together:
Pray with your spouse and ask for the Lord's help in always being honest with each other and never pretentious.

51. Sarcasm

Growing Old Together...   By John M. Cimbala, 2019

Frank: I think I'll go downtown and get a haircut.
Ethel: (looking closely at Frank's head) Why stop at *one*? You should get *all twelve* of your hairs cut. ☺
Frank: ☹
Ethel: ☺
Frank: ☹

Artwork by Helen Dickey

Now the men who were holding Jesus in custody were mocking him as they beat him. They also blindfolded him and kept asking him, "Prophesy! Who is it that struck you?
Luke 22:63-64 (ESV)

Read Together:
Is sarcasm ever okay in marriage? The definition of **sarcasm** is "a mode of satirical wit directed against an individual; the use of irony to mock or convey contempt; a sneering or cutting remark." I mistakenly thought that sarcasm was a tool for humor, much like *teasing* or *satire*. From the above definition, however, sarcasm is actually more hurtful, harsh, and cutting than I had previously realized. As evidenced by these devotionals, I appreciate humor. Teasing can be part of harmless humor, as in today's comic. We need to be careful, however, that our teasing is not hurtful and does not turn into sarcasm. Although I could not find any Bible verses that use the word "sarcasm," there are plenty of verses that use the words "mock" or "mocking." Today's introductory scripture passage describes the (unfair) trial and mocking of Jesus before those who had arrested him. They blindfolded and struck him and then asked mockingly who hit him. This kind of mocking is sarcasm at its ugliest. I can't help but be deeply hurt for Jesus' suffering as he silently endured this hateful mockery. At the same time, though, I am eternally grateful that he, ridiculed and rebuffed, suffered and died in *my* place, to pay for *my* sins.

As Jesus Christ himself said in **John 15:13**, *"Greater love has no one than this, that someone lay down his life for his friends."* May we have this same attitude toward *our* friends, and especially toward our *spouse*.

Gently teasing your spouse is okay sometimes if done in love and if both of you find it humorous. But be careful that your teasing is not *hurtful* and never turns into *sarcasm* as you grow old together.

Discuss Together:
1. I have observed that men tend to tease more than women, often to the point of sarcasm. Discuss whether or not you agree, and why.
2. Discuss where each of you draws the line between humorous, harmless teasing and hurtful, cutting sarcasm. If that line differs greatly between the two of you, discuss ways to keep from crossing your spouse's line.
3. Think of times when teasing or light-hearted joking by your spouse, though not ill-intended, was hurtful. Discuss how you felt at the time and how the situation could (should) have been handled differently.
4. Re-read today's introductory scripture passage. What do you learn about *grace* from this account of the contemptible sarcasm inflicted on our Savior, Jesus Christ?
5. The gospel is about grace and forgiveness. Forgive each other for those times when teasing, though intended for humor, turned hurtful and sarcastic.

Study Together:
Study **2 Kings 19:8-37**, the account of King Sennacherib of Assyria as he and his army prepared to destroy Jerusalem and mocked God by boasting about his victories over neighboring nations. Discuss how this must have made the people of Jerusalem, including King Hezekiah, feel. Read Isaiah's prophecy in answer to Hezekiah's prayer and what ultimately happened to the sarcastic Assyrian king. With the Lord's help, you will never intentionally use sarcasm to hurt someone, especially your spouse, whom you should love and cherish.

Pray Together:
Pray with your spouse and ask for the Lord's help in not crossing the line from harmless teasing to hurtful sarcasm.

52. Absentmindedness

Laugh Together:

Growing Old Together...   By John M. Cimbala, 2019

Frank: (reflecting) I think you're right. I guess I *am* getting more absentminded.

Ethel: Why do you say that?

Frank: I thought of a really good idea for my Growing Old Together series.

Ethel: And you forgot what it was?

Frank: No, I looked back and saw that I already posted it two weeks ago! ...☺

Artwork by Helen Dickey

Bless the Lord, O my soul, and forget not all his benefits.
Psalm 103:2 (ESV)

Read Together:

Are you becoming absentminded? The definition of ***absentmindedness*** is "having or showing a habitually forgetful or inattentive disposition; forgetful; oblivious." I am guilty as charged. I often find myself forgetting to do something because I am in deep thought about something totally unrelated. It sometimes upsets my wife, and she tells me I am the classic "absentminded professor." She wishes I would do better in this area, and I *try*, but absentmindedness is not easily corrected, and it is getting worse as I age. Not too much harm is done if we forget to buy something or forget that we had posted something on Facebook a few weeks ago, as in today's comic. But when it comes to remembering our Lord God, we cannot afford to be absentminded! Today's introductory scripture passage reminds us not to forget all the benefits from our Lord. And what are these benefits? The psalmist lists some of them in the next few verses: the Lord forgives your iniquity, heals your diseases, redeems your life from the pit, crowns you with steadfast love and mercy, and satisfies you with good so that your youth is renewed like the eagle's. I agree with the first few benefits on this list but am not so convinced about that last one. My youth is gone and will not be renewed until I step into glory. It is also inevitable that both you and your spouse will become more absentminded as you grow old together. Give him or her some slack, though, since it is not intentional. As today's introductory scripture passage reminds us, do not forget all the Lord's benefits.

Give grace to your spouse as you grow old together and you *both* become more absentminded. Treasure the memories you have.

Discuss Together:
1. Discuss your attitude about becoming more absentminded. Do you laugh it off? Does it scare you? How can you arrive at a balance between the humor and fear of absentmindedness?
2. Think of and discuss an instance when you or your spouse did something absentmindedly that turned out to be funny. Laugh together as you look back at this event and its consequences.
3. Similarly, discuss an episode of absentmindedness that caused fear, harm, or hurt feelings; that was *not* a laughing matter. Discuss how you might have handled the situation differently. Discuss practical ways to avoid similar situations in the future.
4. Discuss times of great joy and satisfaction from earlier years in your marriage. As you reminisce about these times, hold hands and thank the Lord for your spouse.
5. The gospel is about grace and forgiveness. Forgive each other for the times you have forgotten to do or say something that may have worried your spouse or hurt his or her feelings.

Study Together:
Study **Psalm 119:89-112**, David's psalm about his heartfelt love for God's Word (or Law in some translations). Count how many times David vows never to *forget* the Word of the Lord in this brief portion of this famous psalm. Discuss how much more *we* should thank the Lord and forget not his Word. With the Lord's help, as you become more absentminded with age, you will never forget God's Word.

Pray Together:
Pray with your spouse. Ask for the Lord's help in forgiving your spouse as he or she becomes more absentminded with age. After all, it is not intentional and is happening or will happen to you as well.

Final Bookend. Valley

Final Devotional (not a laughing matter):

Growing Old Together...

By John M. Cimbala, 2019

Frank: (as Ethel returns from the doctor's office) What did he say?

Ethel: (in tears) He gave me six months.

Frank: (choking up) How are we going to deal with this?

Ethel: The way we have always dealt with difficulties...

Frank: Together.

Ethel: Yes. Together.

Artwork by Helen Dickey

Even though I walk through the valley of the shadow of death, I will fear no evil, for you are with me; your rod and your staff, they comfort me.
Psalm 23:4 (ESV)

Read Together:

The first and last devotionals in this book are "bookends." The first one was foundational. This last one puts all the previous ones in perspective.

This final devotional is the most serious – definitely the most difficult one I had to write. The definition of *valley* is "the low place between two heights; a low point or condition." Inevitably, we must all walk through the valley of the shadow of death, as in today's introductory scripture passage. In this most famous and beloved of Psalms, David relates how he is comforted by visualizing God as a shepherd, guiding him with rod and staff through the valley of death. Discussing your own death, or the death of your spouse, can be emotionally heart wrenching. Unless you die together in some sort of accident, it is likely one of you will be taken from this earth before the other. You or your spouse may have to deal with a terminal illness or Alzheimer's. Some of you may already be going through this, or you may have gone through it in a previous marriage. For others, the death of your spouse may come suddenly and without warning. Although it may be awkward and painful, discussing death with your spouse and thinking about how the one who remains will deal with life thereafter can prove beneficial. There is comfort in knowing the one you love will be in a better place, with Jesus, with no more tears or suffering. Yet, for the spouse left behind, loneliness, pain, uncertainty, times of depression, and maybe even anger or guilt may be present. Even with strong Christian faith, healing takes time. I imagine this is especially true for those who have been married a long time.

Enjoy the time you have and have had with your spouse as you grow old together. Make good memories together now because someday those memories may be all that remain.

Discuss Together:
1. Have you discussed with your spouse how to deal with the death of one of you? Take some time now to share your feelings and fears.
2. Affirm your love for each other by sharing what you would miss most about your spouse if he or she dies before you.
3. Discuss some practical ways to prepare yourselves for the death of you or your spouse: what kind of funeral you want, your finances, which friends or family members you can turn to for help, etc.
4. Is it selfish to want to die *before* your spouse? Is it selfish to want to die *after* your spouse?
5. The gospel is about grace and forgiveness. Forgive each other in advance in case *you* are the one who leaves the other behind.

Study Together:
Study **2 Timothy 4:7-8**, where the Apostle Paul writes about having fought the good fight, having finished the race, having kept the faith, and looking forward to the crown of righteousness which the Lord will reward to him. Discuss how this scripture passage comforts you as you ponder death. With the Lord's help, you can have joy in the midst of your sorrow as you visualize a crown of righteousness on the head of your spouse.

Pray Together:
Pray with your spouse. Ask for the Lord's help in dealing with illnesses and end-of-life issues. Comfort each other and renew your covenant to go through these and other issues together... till death parts you.

About the Author

John M. Cimbala was born in 1957 in Pittsburgh, PA. After graduating from Norwin High School in North Huntingdon, PA, he attended Penn State, where he earned his BS in Aerospace Engineering in 1979. He then went to Caltech in Pasadena, CA, where he earned his MS in Aeronautics in 1980. He married his college sweetheart Suzy that same year and then she helped him earn his PhD in Aeronautics in 1984. Since then, he has served on the faculty of Penn State as Professor of Mechanical Engineering, teaching and conducting research. He and Suzy raised two sons, Andy and Luke Cimbala. At the time of this writing, he has two grandchildren, but he hopes for several more.

John is a devoted Christian who yearns to please the Lord Jesus Christ. He has taught youth and adult Sunday School for more than three decades, and has posted his Bible studies, articles, and devotionals online from his many years of preparing Bible lessons. These and other resources are available on a website that John created and maintains called Christian Faith Grower at www.christianfaithgrower.com. He prays that these free Christian resources will be used for small-group and/or individual Bible study.

John has also written two Biblical historical fiction novels:

- *I, Adam: The Man without a Navel* (https://goo.gl/69NdED)
- *I, Peter: My Life in Threes* (https://goo.gl/ZcTjHy)

Professionally, John has co-authored several textbooks, including one on indoor air quality engineering, a book about renewable energy, and a popular fluid mechanics textbook that is now in its fourth edition, is used around the world, and has been translated into eight foreign languages. All of his professional books can be found at his Amazon Author Page at https://goo.gl/khDWFJ.

John's desire is that this present devotional book will encourage couples to think more deeply about their relationship with each other and to discuss together some of the important issues raised in the devotional readings and discussion questions. He prays that this book will prompt many to read and study the Bible more carefully and regularly, for in it are the Words of Life.

If you have comments or questions about this book, please write to John Cimbala at jmc6@psu.edu.

Growing Old Together...

By John M. Cimbala, 2019

Suzy: (sits down) I'm exhausted!
John: (stands up) Ooo! My back hurts when I stand up!
Suzy: Growing old is not much fun, is it?
John: No... but I am sure glad of one thing.
Suzy: What is that?
John: That we are *growing old together*! ♥...☺
Suzy: Yes! *Together*! ☺...♥

Made in the USA
Columbia, SC
11 January 2021

30736761R00065